Lost
in the
Clouds

Leenda B Mac

ISBN 978-1-63575-346-2 (Paperback)
ISBN 978-1-64079-242-5 (Hard Cover)
ISBN 978-1-63575-347-9 (Digital)

Christian Faith Publishing, Inc.
296 Chestnut Street
Meadville, PA 16335
www.christianfaithpublishing.com

Printed in the United States of America

Contents

Acknowledgment and Dedication

To all those who believed in my dire effort of getting this manuscript going in a right direction and continued to keep me going to pursue my writing mission, I thank you so much!

My editors—First Officer Andy and his lovely wife, Marcia, Joel, loving and inspiring friend Patricia.

Front cover designed by my fellow Captain Nick, an awesome photographer.

My Denver based coworkers, administration, headquarters, ground personnel, former airline associates, loving family, friends, passengers, adorable children, Jason, Jeffrey, Joel, Shannon, and my precious grandbabies. May they always continue to inspire a "spark" of writing inside of my heart and soul!

Cheers to all of you who have brought this book into a final completion. I can't thank you enough.

Due to your continuous support, love, and encouragement in making this dream come true, I love all of you and will be forever grateful for all you've taught me in life's journey. May each day remain an incredible gift to bestow with our treasured beauty in life!

Blessings and peace,
Leenda

Introduction

I WROTE THIS SERIES OF SHORT STORIES for you to comprehend what a crew member entails while in the air and of service as a road warrior. It's never an easy tranformation with our job requirements; although I must admit our cycle of influence is tremedous in what we can accomplish. Providing a sense of hope, love, faith, and laughter for our guests traveling the highway in the sky is a worthy mission. May this gift of writing inspire your innermost soul as it has for myself in my job capacity! My goal is to keep you laughing in our every moment of toil and faltered measures we contend with.

My Flight Academy

WHILE HOLDING DOWN SEVERAL JOBS IN DENVER at golf courses, restaurants, a bowling center, care provider for disabled adults, and cleaning homes for extra cash, I was growing weary of my direction in life. I came across an advertisement for a Flight Attendant with Angel Air and decided to head to a job fair in downtown Denver. Upon my arrival, I was curious with many vendors promoting opportunities for their company. Nothing seemed to stir my soul until I was guided to the Angel Air booth. I picked up information regarding the available times and dates for a group interview. My ex-airline friends were thrilled when I informed them I attended this function. They told me, "Go for it!"

After tossing this around in my head, I decided to give it a shot for I had nothing to lose. I got up early to fight the traffic for my group interview. I got lost several times, trying to locate the hotel, and uttered a fervent prayer. God brought me right to the front door without bashing someone's car and looking like a "lost soul." I entered with much poise, decked out in my Sunday business suit, looking very polished, even though I was nervous. I was the oldest participant, and I needed to restore my confidence as it had been several years since I had been active in the airline business. Being a Flight Attendant, however, was brand-new to me. These fresh faces were slightly intimidating on the surface, but I knew that between my airline experience and customer service skills, I had a great shot!

We were briefed with the company background, history, and future outlook—which is always invigorating. Then we were asked one by one to answer a question in front of the group: "Why do you want to be a Flight Attendant with Angel Air?" I heard enough "sweet or sour" answers to make me cringe or cheer for one another's response. Nevertheless, we were all searching for employment with a worthy company. When it was my turn to answer this question, I gave a solid answer: "Probably because I've done everything within this business except fly the plane or be a Flight Attendant." The crowd came to a hush with my remark. Gazing around at these young, vigorous faces searching for a rainbow in the sky, I came to the conclusion that maybe they didn't want to hire an "old-timer" like me. Possibly, they're searching for a fresh look minus the laughter lines I had accrued over the years. I submitted my résumé, had a personal interview, and shook a few hands on my way out. I gave it my best attempt, walking out of the hotel with much pride in my accomplishment. If I passed the test, they would contact me.

After five days had passed with no word in the mail or e-mail, I took off to apply at other places. How I dreaded another time of being out on a limb with no work due to a seasonal job at a golf course. When I arrived back home, I had a phone message. Angel Air had informed me of my acceptance into the flight academy, when I needed to report for duty, and my homework arriving in the mail. I danced around my living room, singing Helen Reddy's favorite tune "I Am Woman." Wow! This was the best Christmas gift I could've asked for under my tree. Now, could I retain information to conquer my studies? I hope so. I may have to load up on Ginkgo, but I'm proud and willing to accept this assignment.

So there I was, on my way to training in Salt Lake City, Utah, during the cold, bitter winter month of January. It was a crucial time of "weeding out the good, bad, and indifferent." I was diligent in my studies, hitting the books every night while practicing our announcements with my roommate, Natalie. There were times we sponsored a pajama party in our room to critique one another. Elizabeth brought the snacks to rev up our energy. Observing the new employees coming into the training center, it brought back memories of my days serving as a cheerleading and dance team moderator. There was energy, excitement, and perpetual "jitters," as we all knew we were in the same boat.

Due to hard work effort, I passed all my required testing, received my wings, and was set to graduate the end of January. I was one beaming lady, knowing I didn't give up the fight. Most of our class received Salt Lake City as their primary city of operation. It was time to go home, pack up my gear, and head on down the highway. I may have been a rookie at the time, but I planned to learn from my fellow coworkers on how in-flight duty in the airline business was a whole different ball game than working on the ground. Here I go!

My IOE

DEPARTING ON MY TRIP SERIES WITH CAPTAIN John, First Officer Josh, fellow Flight Attendant Nathan, and my instructor Melissa, I was apprehensive in passing my final testing. This is a requirement after you've finished graduating from our flight academy. We were dealing with weather problems in Aspen, Colorado, although we made an attempt to make it. Unfortunately, the weather turned sour, and we were forced to return to Denver, Colorado. We tried it again. While on route the second time, I had to rehearse my required duties and proper announcements. Suddenly, there was an outburst coming through the flight deck, "AHHHHH," once we landed. Little did I know, we just missed going off the runway by a foot due to snow, ice, and windy conditions.

Now, is this any way to start off a new career, hanging off a mountaintop? I contemplated.

It becomes a snowball effect when flights run tardy. We do our best to make up for the delay in the air, but it depends on wind, visibility, and proper landing conditions. Weather is a major factor we deal with for the safety of our passengers. Enabling their needs once they get onboard is a huge responsibility after fielding many of their emotions. It's part of the job to keep our passengers happy. I understand their frustrating moments, but think about our endeavor trying to land in one piece—let alone, I'm a rookie on my IOE, better known as my initial operating experience. What a way to start off! Once we landed into Aspen, we had to head to Chicago, Illinois. Due to misconnections, we had to ferry the flight into Chicago, which meant an empty aircraft.

The next day we headed back into Aspen but once again could not land due to weather conditions. Therefore, we flew into Grand Junction, Colorado, as an alternate. We made arrangements to have our passengers escorted via a bus into Aspen, and then we left for Los Angeles, California. Once again we had to ferry an empty aircraft into California. When we arrived into Los Angeles, we had a full ship going into San Diego, California. If this is my initiation as a crew member, it certainly has started off with a "detour." My fellow crew members kept me laughing over my IOE—although due to lack of passenger service, I did have to repeat the process the following week to complete my IOE. All I can say is, "Welcome aboard!"

Shhh . . . Do Not Disturb

IN EDMONTON, CANADA, CAPTAIN ROD, FIRST OFFICER Dwane, and myself decided to dine on some refreshing treats. Knowing it was Saint Patrick's Day, my Irish background craved for some corn beef, cabbage, and a green toast. We were not sure the Canadians celebrated this event, but we gave it a try. However, we found a pizza place and munched on some pasta instead. Sigh . . . so much for my green event. We had an early show in the morning, so we were dedicated employees in bed by eight at night. All of us got woken up at 3:15 a.m. due to some party animals and teens laughing and yelling in the hallway. Our parental instinct kicked in as we opened our doors at the same time, scolding these teens for waking us up, claiming they were interfering with our rest. They were paralyzed with fear, listening to our shouting match in the beginning hours of the morning. With an apology, they slipped away in a silent mode. After we accomplished our task, we glanced at one another in our nighttime apparel. The First Officer, whose hair is normally very well groomed and sleeked to his head, was now a shock of spiked wheat. I couldn't help but comment on his bad "bed head" look.

He stared at me and replied, "Well, you don't exactly have a teddy on my dear," as I was dressed in my flannel pants, booties, and sweatshirt.

The Captain joined in with his response, "Makeup works miracles in the morning, doesn't it, Leenda?"

OK, now I was outnumbered. It was two against one.

I told the Captain, "Well, sir, you'll never make *GQ Magazine* dressed in your silly Joe Boxer's and Snoopy T-shirt."

We started laughing so hard and continued to slam one another with our behind-the-scene appearance minus our uniforms. Closing the doors, I could still hear the Captain laughing through the hotel walls. We chuckled until our alarms went off at 3:45 a.m. Time to get up and look professional, even though this will be another short night of crew rest. It was a "top of the morning" to remember on our Canadian Saint Patrick's Day trip series!

To Commute Is a Challenge

I'VE HAD THE PLEASURE OF MEETING MANY flight crew members who commute to their home base with an assignment. It's a breath-holding event when attempting to catch a flight and be to work on time. I've already dealt with this anguish, trying to get to my home in Denver, Colorado, from Salt Lake City, Utah. I've discovered living in an airport all day on your day off is not an inviting experience. Sweating bullets in the gate area to see if you can make it home and return for your trip series can be an incredible, worrisome, and weary task. It becomes a game of chess—watching, waiting, and wondering if the king or queen of seniority will knock the pawns off the game board. It can feel helpless, but I have learned to make new gate agent friends. I understand this tactic since I used to be an agent. I had many commuters showering me with chocolate to make sure they were placed early on the standby list. Sometimes it worked, and other times it didn't.

I've learned to stay in a mode of acceptance. Stress doesn't accomplish anything. If I get the boot in the gate area, I simply stay in silence and hope for an available seat on the next flight. It usually transpires if I remain in a motion of stillness. We all take care of one another in-flight. It's an enjoyable time for me to meet fellow crew members from all different airline companies. We do our best to accommodate one another, for we have the same job responsibility and acknowledge the pain of getting to our destiny. It's a riot to share stories regarding our in-flight troubles and our vigilant effort to get to our flight before time expires. We'll sprint from one airline to another to tackle business. We know how to get our human bowling ball rolling down a concourse. Our mind-set alters as we view passengers like many bowling pins in an alley. We don't intend to knock you over for a strike or spare—although when we have to report to work, it's wise to stand aside or you'll end up in the gutter. Commuting crew members can be a hazardous bunch of characters aimed at getting to their flight and gate for their assigned departure. Most passengers are accommodating with our need to slip through the front lines with security screening. Once in a while, you hear a discontented passenger complain that we cut in front of the line. Our TSA friends have to remind them, "This maybe your possible crew flying the aircraft you're about to take. You're not going anywhere until they get to their plane to conduct business, so lighten up!" Hats off to our TSA friends for providing an answer on our behalf. We are constantly on alert for one other, for we all know the strife in this industry.

Call us a bizarre bunch of individuals, but we are a group continually running a marathon in airports, bus stops, traffic, or weather hassles when it comes to serving our jobs. Even though our showtime is urgent, we do our best to be on time. No wonder we have a caring ear for a tattered passenger, for we've probably already been there, done that. Many of us have not started a trip series with an eight-hour day, but more like a twelve- or thirteen-hour day. When we arrive to our hotel room on day 1, we collapse. A long layover to get regrouped for the next day is a welcome treasure to catch up on lack of sleep. That does not always take place, but we are grateful for a time-out. Dealing with weather, turbulence, irate passengers, excess baggage onboard can rise the blood pressure. We simply do our best with a pleasant greeting despite our effort to get on our aircraft before our passengers. To attempt a healthy lifestyle can be impossible due to our wild and hectic schedules. Sometimes our breakfast, lunch, and dinner consists of pretzels, crackers, or peanuts when we have no time to eat or dip into our lunch bags. To dine on a peanut butter and jelly sandwich at 6:45 a.m. can be your only hope of sustaining energy until the next destination where you can hopefully locate a microwave oven. That's our on-the-move lifestyle.

In the meantime, to accept this wayward lifestyle—living like a gypsy in a suitcase—is not for everyone. It takes a lot of energy to retain stamina as a crew member. For most of us in this business, we learn to adjust, laugh, and devise a new plan of attack to get to work. We are troopers, so stay on guard when you witness a uniformed crew member plowing through the airport with our black bags. Our heels will be clicking as a warning signal. We will mow you over to get to our flight on time. That's how we operate.

"Love Taps"

DEALING WITH OVERSIZE BAGGAGE ONBOARD IS ONE task; although handling an oversize passenger is another issue. A gentleman traveling from Pasco, Washington, to Phoenix, Arizona, took up two seats on the aircraft. He was very self-conscious of his limitations and inability to navigate around the small space of the aircraft. He asked if he could move up front due to his short connection.

"Hmmm, let me see what I can find for you, sir," I replied.

Understanding my choices were limited, it was necessary to locate two open seats together. Sure enough, seats 2A and B were available. I went to the rear of the aircraft to inform my passenger that I could move him to the front to better his situation. He let out a huge moan to achieve a standing position. Due to his size, he had to turn sideways to move his way down the narrow center aisle. During his attempt, his stomach hit passengers in the face on aircraft's right and his rear end slapped passengers on aircraft's left. Situated in the forward galley, I watched this gentleman slowly work his way toward the front of the aircraft. His effort was a tiresome journey but a diligent one. I observed many reactions onboard. Some were giggling; others rolled their eyes or uttered a scowl of disgust. Suddenly, in a cheerful mode, this man blurted out, "It's nothing but a love tap, nothing but a love tap."

I was amazed and in awe of his lighthearted disposition, giving him a round of applause. I felt like a cheerleader in the sky, rooting him onto victory to cross the finish line in getting a forward seat. His attitude was a reflection of his innermost genuine spirit. We place much emphasis in our society on the exterior appearance. This man dealt with his obesity issues in a manner to be commended. His dose of a "Fat Albert" cartoon made me smile. All I can say is, "Hey, hey, hey!" No matter what mushrooms onboard due to limited space on our regional aircraft, I enjoy teaching passengers how to create a unique travel experience. You can choose to whine, complain, and judge the person seated next to you. However, my thought is, *Why not make a new friend during your flight regardless of how they look?* You may deal with an oversize individual sneaking a silent moment to ask for an extension belt, but the formula in dealing with this issue is one of kindness, compassion, and conversation. It's an amazing technique to be open to all personalities, no matter what size nor gender. People have an opportunity to learn from one another traveling city to city. I could probably use an extension belt on my jump seat from eating many airport meals loaded with sodium and unnecessary carbohydrates. I have my bloating moments. It is possible my saturated lunch pail needs to load up with more fruits and veggies to get me through my next four-day trip. We will see. I still like a good burger and fries every now and then. In the meantime, I will pass on my personal "love taps."

Through the Storm

MY FOUR-DAY TRIP IN MAY SERVING AS a new hire Flight Attendant for Angel Air was not only a test on the EMB but a comedy of errors. Our assignment began in Denver, Colorado. Captain Cliff, First Officer Mason, and I departed Denver in May 2007. Leaving for a few local short trips within the region, we were prepared. Knowing we were dealing with springtime storms, we were set for a round of turbulence according to the weather report—not to mention, a full moon played havoc on our series of trips to Grand Junction, Colorado; Casper, Wyoming; Rapid City, South Dakota; and Montrose, Colorado.

We contended with 60-mph winds, thunderstorms, tornado clouds, torrential rain, and several lightning bolts from above. This little thirty-passenger aircraft got tossed from every direction. My beverage service came to an abrupt halt several times as I barely made it back to my jump seat for safety purposes. The Captain was in constant touch to inform me of inclement weather. A group of burly men, traveling back to Rapid City from Denver after delivering a stage set for a well-known actor, sat like a cozy family in the rear of the aircraft. They rang my Flight Attendant button.

"What do you need? I've been instructed to sit in my jump seat."

His reply was, "We want a few cocktails."

"You've got to be joking", I muttered to myself.

"Just roll it down the center aisle, honey, like you're on a bowling lane."

My answer back was, "Here comes a gutter ball."

I was amazed at their silly request despite the raging storm, but we kept the humor flying on route to Rapid City. After arriving, we had a quick turn back to Denver. How I dreaded the trip back. I could only pray.

Bouncing from seat to seat and assisting passengers was a challenge. I received bumps on my head from overhead bins and gained a few unfortunate bruises maintaining my stand in the aisle. It was a chore. Arriving into Denver, we were at the gate, waiting to board passengers, when we witnessed a huge lightning bolt illuminating the sky. Ramp personnel disappeared immediately due to unsafe conditions. Our crew remained onboard and faithfully had to wait out the impending storm. Captain Cliff made a decision to watch a few taped DVDs on his laptop computer until the ground stop expired at Denver. Why not? Mason and I got exposed to *Jackass* in the flight deck. We laughed so hard at this offbeat scene, for it served as a great stress reducer.

We were finally ready to board after the storm passed, although another unfortunate incident occurred. A ramp agent left checked baggage on an open cart forward of the wing. Like children after Christmas gifts under a tree, passengers noticed their checked bags while boarding and decided to plunge into their bag of goodies after being screened. Whoops! That's a breach in security. Here comes the cavalry with TSA, director of security operations, flashing red lights, and a bus to deplane and escort our passengers back to rescreening. Passengers were furious, although TSA were only doing their job for security maneuvers. Our crew had to do another security check within the aircraft as we normally do for a procedural first flight of the day. Now we have to conduct this project once again. Passengers felt like criminals while expressing their rampant emotions toward us. Maybe a fire hose would come in handy to cool off their hostile nature. We don't appreciate turning into an airport warden, but it's our responsibility to abide by the rules. To appease their anger, our passengers were compensated by a travel voucher to pacify their inconvenience.

Returning to our aircraft for reboarding, I was informed it was Cinco de Mayo weekend.

"How about a few free margaritas and tacos onboard for all of us?"

I paused on my response. "Si, senor. My taco machine is getting repaired. How about a pretzel dipped in salsa with a glass of water to quench your thirst?"

This got the crowd fired up with giggles instead of concentrating on their unfortunate mishap or hanging me off the side of the plane with my demo mask.

It takes a lot within to calm down a storm from the outside as well as the inside. Being in the airline business for several years, I've learned a new method. It's called laughter. This seems to be effective in battling heartless behavior on the ground as well as in the air. Nothing seems to astonish me with passenger requests. Learning the in-flight portion is another test of endurance. My question is, "Are we having fun yet?"

On route to Grand Junction, we were informed of another ground stop in Denver. Ugh! It gave us more time to watch more *Jackass* adventures on Cliff's DVD player in the flight deck. We had tears rolling down our faces from giggling with this ludicrous series. To promote good humor onboard is an asset and a vital need. Once again, this was a devoted crew I was blessed with. Serving as a Flight Attendant to overcome many obstacles is a zealous effort. Thank goodness, we have many devoted employees. I continue to appreciate a team forced together in the name of doing our job with the utmost diligence and professionalism. We're constantly dealing with risky circumstances, but the manner we tackle a perilous situation for the safety of our passengers is our top priority. They may not understand nor appreciate our decisions, although when they arrive in a safe means, peek out a window to view the weather conditions, it's a somber moment. Every once in a while, I'd love to express, "We told you so, but you didn't listen in your panic mode or anxiety attack with your connections." However, I remain quiet in my thoughts. We race against the clock nonstop to provide proper connection time, yet we deal with obstacles. May we remain on a safe course through the storms and on a journey in life with a purpose.

Angel Onboard

I LEFT FROM DENVER IN MAY 2007 with Captain Matt and First Officer Laura for a four-day trip series. It was an innocent beginning in serving our passengers. Our obligation consisted of Denver, Colorado; Lincoln, Nebraska; Chicago, Illinois; and Appleton, Wisconsin, for our first day. We were held up in Lincoln over four hours due to weather in Chicago. Laura and I made the best of the situation by hanging out in Operations, watching the movie *Airplane*, while our Captain camped out in the aircraft to catch up on some rest coming in from Orlando. We laughed at Matt turning our aircraft into his personal "pup tent," with his long legs draped over the side of the aisle seat, yearning for a blackout impression by drawing all the shades to a close for a quick snooze. Chicago was finally free from the thunder boomers. We received clearance, so off we flew. Arriving in Chicago, you could feel the after-effects of the storm. We had to be patient dealing with ground service as they were short-staffed and didn't expect this spontaneous cloud burst. Dealing with fatigue, we still managed to provide and assist our customers with proficient service. We were worn down.

We made it into Appleton, Wisconsin, late and dropped in our hotel beds. Up early the next day, we left for Chicago; Roanoke, Virginia; Chicago, and back to Lexington, Kentucky. It was another mission with bad weather. My jump seat got a quivering workout. I'm wearing out the Good Lord's precious ears with all my requests for a safe arrival once again. I was so relieved to have my feet on the ground. We had an opportunity to kick up our crew heels in Lexington and explore the fine hospitality this city provides. We met several locals who shared their Irish shenanigans with us. It was a grand event.

I suppose we needed this time-out as we endured an incredible adventure the next day. Leaving Chicago on route to Winnipeg, Canada, I heard a terrible explosion in the front galley after I finished my service. I knew it wasn't the engines, but it sounded like a lawn mower or chainsaw. I contacted Matt and asked what's going on. He informed me, "I'll get back to you." Our ADG—which is a backup generator for power—deployed, leaving us not in a state of emergency but a needed diversion for maintenance. That's not an easy prognosis when you are thirty-three thousand feet in the air. The noise was tremendous. Matt contacted our passengers to put them at ease. I dealt with nail-biting and nervous behavior inside the cabin.

Passengers were flipping out on me due to the piercing racket in the front of the aircraft. Some were crying, others were praying, and the majority were hanging on for dear life, frightened from the intense sound and immobilized with fear.

A passenger yelled out, "We're going to die because we're going down."

I calmly looked at him and replied, "No, we are not, sir."

I was amazed at my basic training, which kicked into gear at the most necessary moment. Remaining composed (even though my heart was racing, knees shaking, and hands trembling), I maintained for the sake of my passengers. I had to assist and alleviate any alarm. I noticed a seven-month-old baby in the rear of the aircraft. He had warm, beautiful brown eyes filled with a tranquil sense of peace. He simply smiled at me. As I stared at this young infant, his innocent smile gave me much comfort to carry on my responsibilities. If this was my moment to yodel into heaven, I think I did a pretty good job asking the Good Lord for a safe arrival to Minneapolis, Minnesota, for all of us. This little babe gave me the motivation to continue with perseverance, courage, and hope. I'll never forget this moment.

Remember, when in trouble, there's always an innocent angel to protect you. That's an encouraging thought.

We landed unharmed in Minneapolis. We had to wait for another aircraft to be delivered for us to take passengers to Winnipeg and still venture back to Chicago. We hugged one another as crew members, knowing we did our job to the best of our ability. My Captain, Matt, and First Officer Laura handled this problem with much composure. I was proud to be a part of this crew. They are to be commended for their faithful journey in the eyes of safety for our Angel Air passengers onboard. I must admit: I've had a few post-trauma flashbacks due to this event—although I know the angels were looking over this flight crew.

When you're in an emergency situation for others remain steadfast and confident. It's not a time of hysteria, for all innocent eyes are looking at you as a leader to provide a safety net and a secure landing. This is when you become a warrior for others. Your mind can be in a tangled swirl in the moment, but it's a natural instinct to be prepared, to protect, and to provide. This is a prime example of being a soldier in the air. Never give up the effort for the sake of others and always thank your angels for a guarded flight in the air. I continue to proudly wear an angel pin on my uniform. It's a constant reminder of whose wings are an important and integral asset in airline travel.

A Smelly Flight

WHEN THE COMPANY IS IN NEED, WE as crew members rise to the occasion. Sitting in reserve duty at Denver, I was called out to Los Angeles, California, in June to meet up with a Tucson crew short of a Flight Attendant. Traveling to Los Angeles, I noticed many passengers scolding gate agents due to oversold situations, late flights, missed connections, excess carry-on items to take onboard, crying babies, and those in wheelchairs needing additional assistance. I remember the days serving in this area of the airline industry. I've already performed that job on the ground level. Welcome to summertime travel. It takes a lot of endurance to serve on the ground as well as in the air. Giving a quick wink to those on ground assisting many needs was an added perk of encouragement to inform them we're a team effort to keep motivated, create a smile, and keep a thumbs-up attitude despite unfortunate problems.

Meeting with my crew in Los Angeles was another great challenge. We shook hands, received our briefing, and resolved any upcoming information to share with one another. Handling another full flight with infants positioned on the wrong side of the aircraft, overweight passengers needing seat belt extensions, and traveling with oversize baggage is quite a task before departure. Most of the passengers are pretty receptive and friendly as they board the aircraft, although there's always a robust individual to stir up the pot based on their personal encounter with their past airline travel times.

I remain firm with any decisions I need to make for the safety of our passengers. Any disputation can be overcome with responsive deeds. A tense nature will attempt to uproot a tranquil experience. There are always times to put out the flicker before it turns into a raging blaze of sensation onboard.

Traveling from Los Angeles to San Jose, California, was another story. I had two young men who were fresh off the beach after surfing, with remnants of seaweed still stuck in their shorts dripping on the floor; a young man who asked me to reseat him due to a smelly passenger next to him; along with a mother and daughter seated in the bulk seats who spilled egg salad on their shirts. Lord, help me. I swept up the sand on the galley floor, told the gentleman with his reseating request to turn his head sideways and breathe out of his mouth for it's not a long flight, and gave the gals who smelled like rotten Easter Eggs some sanitary wipes.

During my service, I had a passenger who screamed out, "Madam, madam, please tell this passenger to put his shoes back on, for it smells like dead fish in here."

Oh no. What's next in my job responsibilities?

I suggested, "Why don't you tell him to put his shoes back on, unless you have some Odor Eaters on hand to lend him. Due to the quick duration of this flight, I need to finish my beverage service. I'll appreciate your cooperation."

After we arrived in San Jose, the Captain needed to use the lavatory. Walking back into the cabin, he grasped his nose, exclaiming, "What the heck smells so bad back here?"

I smirked and informed him he had to see it to believe it. Yep, it was a smelly flight all right. I used the lavatory refreshment spray to get the stench out while Captain D opened up the galley service door to get some fresh air in the cabin for the time being before we had to depart again. No wonder we need not only earplugs but nose plugs can be a handy tool when dealing with odors.

I suppose my nose can tolerate nasty funk due to changing diapers over the years raising four children. Childish as it may be, there is a funny notion listening to passengers complaining with their inability to tolerate the ominous cloud in a closed cabin environment. Is it better to kick up a fuss or to lessen the aroma with a giggle, joke and common sense? To alter an unfortunate situation is not always a pleasant crusade, but the capacity within exists. You simply need to tap into your inner sources to re-direct attitudes. I'm amazed at the transformation when I allow my Irish nature to take over. Suddenly their perception on our so-called "teeny-weeny" aircraft has been eliminated due to our level of service. Remember the saying, "Don't judge a book by its cover?" Well don't judge an aircraft by its wing span is my opinion. I might be a whimsical Flight Attendant in my duty series, yet I know how to have fun. I will continue my keen formula while spreading "good news" in the air. This journey was unpredictable, although spending time with my Tucson crew was enjoyable. Ahhh..., the sweet scent of fresh air when the main cabin door gets open is a precious reward. Existing on a silver submarine in the air makes us appreciative.

Unfortunate Accident

My recent trip leaving Denver, Colorado, on reserve in June was once again an incident with Angel Air. Our routing on a trip series with Captain John, First Officer Marcella, and fellow Flight Attendant, Whitney, was another journey. We ventured to Eugene, Oregon, where I had never been before. It was a long layover and finally a joy to spend a few precious moments of viewing the countryside filled with green terrain, fantastic flowers, and the beauty of God's grace on earth. We sat on our hotel deck to take a moment to reflect, laugh, and share some great airline stories in the midst of our travel expeditions.

The next day Marcella and I got up in the morning before our flight departure to San Francisco. We rented bikes to travel along the river. What a great workout we had, despite the bikes looking like we just came out of the Wizard of Oz, with high handlebars and old-fashioned bike seats to contend with. Oh, well. I told Marcella we were missing the basket in front of our bikes to handle "Toto." How we chuckled over the simple things in life—just grateful we had brakes to handle our bike ride. Traveling along the river path, we absorbed the spectacular landscaping in this area. We even snuck into a garden of roses to breathe a toast of beauty in Eugene. What a lovely time to explore this area of the country. We departed for San Francisco then headed to Aspen, Colorado, for our overnight. This was going to be a short nap as we have an early wake-up call. Time to hit the hay.

Boarding the aircraft the next day in the wee hours of the morning, I entailed an unruly first-class passenger. She reeked of alcohol, possibly due to the food and wine festival held in the Rocky Mountains. I'm sure she had many samples over the weekend activity. Her baggage was too large to entail a safe storage of her belongings. I attempted to handle her oversize bag in a kind means.

I requested, "Why don't you allow me to check this bag for you and you may pick it up in Denver when you deplane."

She hissed at me and caught me off guard by tossing her bag on my right foot in the front galley, demanding I take care of business in her behalf.

"Oh, you're just a lousy waitress in the sky," she retorted.

Other passengers were in shock with her comment. Most crew members would've tossed her off immediately. Not me. This Irish chick turns it into a game.

With a sly grin on my face, I responded, "Well, madam, let me give you food for thought. If you go into cardiac arrest onboard, who do you think will revive you? Or worse yet, if a fire breaks out in the cabin, who do you think will be donning the fire, making sure you reach a place of safety? Finally, who do you think will make sure if we have a ditching emergency in water you will be guided out first and myself last? Crew members have other responsibilities other than performing as a waitress in the sky!"

I took my little beverage cart and proudly moved in a forward motion to complete my beverage service. A scowl was still on her face, although I had a round of cheering coming from fellow passengers seated near her. That made my day, although I wanted to scream from the pain endured on my foot, but I continued my duty boarding passengers. I still had to do a round trip back to Denver then on to Birmingham, Alabama. My foot was extremely swollen. I hobbled out of Birmingham's Airport back to Denver the next day. It was an effort.

I contacted crew support. They were gracious to remove me from my final Denver–Fargo, North Dakota, trip. I had to fill out an OJI (on the job injury) and proceeded with much paperwork. I was willing to finish the last leg of the trip, but it was a nice touch to return home and ice my foot.

Working together as a team is an essential element, yet we deal with unexpected behavior at times. My right foot went through a slow healing process, although I must admit it was a painful and crucial attempt to get through this trip and back home to Denver. My flight crew was supportive of my aching foot and could not imagine my ability to continue my service throughout my trip series. I'm a strong bull, but to be caught off guard by this irritable passenger was uncalled for. Together as a crew is an incredible course in life. We learn, assist, and support one another. That's the beauty despite the scoundrels we contend with and the mishaps that may incur. Hobbling home to ice my foot made me reflect on the beauty of having a worthy limb. I've learned to love my working parts and be grateful each and every single day.

A Glamorous Job?

FOR QUITE SOME TIME, I'VE BEEN ASTONISHED as to how passengers look up to crew members strolling through the airport looking sleek and stylish. Little do they comprehend how much time it takes to conquer this look, especially in the early hours with the sun ready to rise. In our rush to catch a van to the airport, we've had our fair share of activities. Here are a few samples:

Coffee spills on our uniform lap due to a wild ride on route to the airport, multiple crews from other airlines jammed into limited space on the hotel van, bags spilling out of the back end, mascara dripping down your face fighting rain, snow, or ice while crossing the tarmac to get to our aircraft, spotting a rip in our nylons due to a bad nail creating a snag, heels getting stuck in the holes of a jet bridge stairway climbing from the outside, lunch pail zippers busting open due to a four-day food supply, surveying for alien creatures hiding under or on top of your hotel bed, no hot water for a morning shower due to construction, malfunctioning hair dryer, so resorting to the heating vent to finish the job, lacking proper heat or cooling in your room due to seasonal changes, stumbling in the dark to conduct a safety check for first flight of the day, preparing pre-flight requirements with your mittens on while utilizing a flash-light due to no ground power, plopping our crew bags in the overhead bins while racing up and down the aisle before passengers climb on to inspect for a suitable entry and worse yet, is finding out the water lines are frozen, so no java. UGH! Not to mention cramming down a bagel with cream cheese dangling off your choppers in the early hours to survive is another class act.

It's incredible how we can polish up the act when we need to. We're not going to be on the front cover of *Glamour* magazine when we appear for our showtime at the airport, yet we put on a good act. We know how to wing it. Please excuse our exhausting accomplishment as we try our best to look presentable, especially when we have to report to work at 5:00 a.m. We're not engaging in a Miss USA celebrity floor show, despite the many crazy things that may go wrong in getting prepared for our flight series. You may not think we care about our personal appearance, but it's a vital cause and good intention before we depart. Can we adjust with the weather changes or hassles in our overnight? Heaven's no. We may have some bad hair days, but we try to administer our passengers with a smile and a safe go with their travel excursion. Our light shines from within instead of the exterior appearance. Isn't this more important in life? I think so.

A Sky-High Celebration

DEPARTING OUT OF DENVER, COLORADO, ON A four-day trip series—
which included my birthday on July 2—I made up my mind: no
matter if I'm working or not, I'm going to enjoy my special day.
Captain Mike and First Officer John were my flight crew members.
We left on July 1 for Burbank, California; San Francisco, California,
and were to overnight in Medford, Oregon. Arriving in after midnight in Medford, a few passengers overheard it was my birthday. I
was flooded with several birthday greetings from passengers. Some
even stopped to give me a hug and thank me for a job well done.
This was a gracious moment. Weary, our team crawled into our hotel
room. All I needed was a bed and a pillow to start my day off.

I woke up in the morning feeling fresh, took a quick hike in
Medford, and enjoyed the beauty of a city I had never visited before.
What a great feeling to be alive, is all I could focus on, and a privilege
to have a job taking me to so many destinations. Leaving Medford,
we were in for a full day of flying. First Officer John made a PA
announcement regarding my birthday.

"Ladies and gentlemen, here's a special wish to our Flight
Attendant Leenda, who is celebrating her thirty-third birthday with
us today."

It's OK to fib a bit regarding your age onboard, I reflected on,
but to have my fellow crew decrease my age by years was a pleasant
gift. More rounds of ovation and good wishes from passengers were

a rare but special treat. On our final trip to Idaho, a group of FBLA students from the area seated in the rear of the aircraft hit the Flight Attendant button. Attending to their needs, a teacher startled me. Informing the students, on the count of 3, the group broke out into a "Happy Birthday" song onboard. I was speechless yet overwhelmed with joy. They applauded my services and gave me numerous birthday hugs. Despite the lack of a traditional birthday cake with candles and ice cream, this was more than enough to make my day complete. Our job consists of many sacrifices. We may not be home for our birthdays, nor special holidays, with our loved ones—although we simply place it on the back burner. We celebrate when we're through with our trip series. Making the best of it with our fellow crewmates and passengers is sufficient. This is our united family in the sky.

We spent the next night in Albuquerque, New Mexico, on July 3 dining on grand Mexican food and beverages. We went to bed early to get some rest before our wake-up call at 4:00 a.m. Snoozing away, we woke up to many bangs. I wondered if it was a holdup in the hotel, yet it was a Fourth of July fireworks display. Gazing out my window, it was a pretty vision; but like my fellow crew members, it was a disruption in our rest. I watched the clock tick away as I knew my 4:00 a.m. wake-up call would be a slow go in the wee hours. Sure enough, my fellow crew members felt the same fatigue in the morning. I had a passenger snoring so loud from Albuquerque to Los Angeles. I felt I could've performed the same rattle in my jump seat with little rest. We managed to maintain our assignment into Los Angeles, California; San Jose, California; back to Los Angeles and Colorado Springs, Colorado; before returning to Denver on the Fourth of July. When you look at the big picture, with fellow crew friends, it certainly was a special birthday celebration after all.

My second birthday experience was with Joseph and Aaron in 2011. We traveled from Santa Barbara, California, Denver, and finally into Palm Springs, California. I had a minor onboard, who used my PA system to wish me a "Happy Birthday." All my passengers sang a "Happy Birthday" tune. This warmed my heart. A passenger who worked in law enforcement offered to pick up my trash. I notified him he didn't have to, yet he insisted due to my birthday.

After he was through collecting and disposing the overflowing trash, a passenger came into the galley and asked him, "By the way, sir, you are running low on paper towels in the lavatory."

He gazed at me in disbelief, yet both of us stared at one another in a giddy manner.

"And I thought I had a hard job," he commented.

When I arrived in Palm Springs, the Renaissance Hotel gave me a special suite as a birthday gift. Boy, oh, boy, it doesn't get any better, in my opinion, with life on the road. What a great time with a special occasion to be grateful for. You learn to always count your blessings!

Snores Onboard

DEPARTING FROM ALBUQUERQUE, NEW MEXICO, TO LOS Angeles, California, a passenger seated in the exit row was obviously a very tired old man. Completing my pretaxi announcement, I ventured to the exit row to give my briefing speech.

He looked at me with dreary eyes and replied, "Yeah . . . whatever. I know your needs, I'll help you out, just leave me alone."

Getting the cabin prepared for take-off, he began to fall into a deep snooze. His snoring started off as a small hum then turned into a major lawn mower. Beginning my beverage service, he became louder as each minute ticked away. I started to giggle as I watched other passengers glaring at me, listening to his annoying clamor. They wanted me to shove a bottle of water in his mouth or use duct tape, but observing him, I realized he was in dire need of sleep. Who knows what job he had to conduct while in this city? Maybe he was in charge of the fireworks display for the Fourth of July. My perception was, this poor man needed to rest. As crew members, we understand the need for *Z*'s. Thank goodness, his room wasn't next to ours the night before, or we would've needed our earplugs all night to get our rest. He was in his own little world, catching flies with his mouth. The brutal vibration became unbearable for other passengers to concentrate on their computers, movies, or playing blackjack. It became an essential duration, attempting to nudge him in the side to cease the snoring, but he never budged. He was lost in a sleepy mode. Nothing more I could do except grin and bear it.

Since this episode, I decided to observe many optional sleeping patterns. I have my own personal stack of funny snoring positions onboard:

1. The Tray Table

Take down the tray table and hover in a forward position to utilize the tray table as your favorite pillow. Not exactly like home sweet home, but a good substitution.

2. The Lean Machine

Drooping in the main aisle like a tree branch weighted down with snow.

3. Breathing on Your Partner's Shoulder

Your breath is hovering like a green cloud over the traveling partner next to you while you snuggle on their shoulder. No, you're not next to your spouse or loved one, and better hope you don't get a slug in the side to startle your cuddling effort.

4. The Placard Effect

Attempting to utilize the placard onboard to shield the shining moment and block out the sun's UV rays on a window seat while sneaking a windowpane snore.

5. The Wide-Mouth Affair

Watching many dentures and cavities exposed due to open-mouth syndrome while snoozing is entertaining. Makes a great ad for dental implants at a dentist's office. Blowing bubbles is another added attraction.

6. The Faultless Grin

Snoozing in a calm mode with a tiny smirk on your face. Must've been a good financial transaction or you won the lotto.

7.   The Head Bobber

You're getting sleepy, very sleepy. Your head is beginning to bob up and down, trying to stay awake, although it's an OZ moment of being lost in the land of "poppies." It's the slick Flight Attendant from the west using her potion to make you go night-night.

8.   The Roving Eyeball

Hearing the fizz of a can opening, the salamander eyeball comes alive. You may pretend to be asleep, but your senses can detect a free beverage service when the cart makes its way down the center aisle. A sluggish eye turns into a roving inspection.

9.   Rock-a-Bye Baby

An opportunity to witness soothing snoozing like a newborn baby in deep slumber. Oh, how we crew members like this vision of calmness and serenity onboard. Makes us want to sing you a lullaby.

10. The Stress Snooze

This is what sounds like a weed eater trimming the front yard. The deeper the snooze, the louder the noise. Our jet engines sound like a purr compared to this human racket.

11. The Leak-Ooze Snooze

This strange sleeping pattern happens when you haven't digested your meal in the nearest airport yet immediately fall asleep in your seat upon take-off. What drools on your chin are a few dangling morsels of what you absorbed. Not an appealing sight, but hope you enjoyed your meal.

12. The Foot-Stomping Snooze

Your iPod is plugged into your ear, and you've got your groove going. Head is rocking to the beat to soothe the mind, and fingers are tapping on your lap. You don't respond to a free beverage as you can't hear me anyway with your eardrums preoccupied with your favorite tunes.

Is snoring any worse than a crying baby onboard? Not really. If Americans traveling think they are inconvenienced on a short flight, try traveling an international flight with this static. You may not appreciate the close quarters, but think of the cozy effect we offer on the aircraft. You'll have the time of your life, for we are a unique group of individuals taking great care of you. We understand silly human behavior patterns. Our goal is to share a safe launch with a touch of amusement along the horizon.

Close Call

MY TRIP WITH CAPTAIN AARON AND FIRST Officer Stacey was another voyage in the sky. Starting off by deadheading to Cedar Rapids, Iowa, to overnight, Stacey and I spent the day with a run for her and a hike for me—observing the countryside. It was an exquisite day in July. I thought we'd be overwhelmed with heat and humidity in the Midwest, but it was a day in the 'seventies. Strolling through Thomas Park and a trail running through the area was a great moment to view people playing volleyball, Frisbee golf, and enjoying a picnic. It was the Midwest. I recalled living in Omaha, Nebraska, for several years, nostalgically reflecting on the amusement in the summertime days with family and friends. After a marveling day, Stacey and I had a bite to eat at a Mexican restaurant then headed back to the hotel to get some rest for our early-morning wake-up call.

We were up at four, getting ready for our trip back to Denver, Colorado; Durango, Colorado; Denver, and Burbank, California. When the alarm clock goes off that early, it is never a failure to let out a gigantic groan, but nonetheless we get prepared for the next day's journey. Thank goodness for Starbucks, for it's a crew member's best friend and energizer bunny in these wee hours of the day. Leaving Cedar Rapids to Denver was a nice flight. Routing from Denver to Durango was another grand excursion. Arriving into Burbank on our final flight, was a warm moment. My uniform was already in a sweaty state due to the heat. Such is life, smelling like Funyuns.

Stacey and I hung at the pool to cool off, swam laps, and enjoyed our special time together.

Departing early again the next morning for Salt Lake City, Utah, there was a wedding reception held in Burbank at our hotel. There was much activity and uproar due to their celebration. In my desperate attempt to get some sleep, it was a strain. I stared bug-eyed at the ceiling, awake for many hours, watching the clock tick by, knowing I had limited hours for rest. I'm sure my fellow coworkers dealt with the same feelings, for the pandemonium was throughout the premises. This is difficult when we deal with rowdy hotel customers and lack of sleep. It goes with the job, but you learn to carry earplugs and do your best to retain "happy thoughts."

We departed the next day from Burbank with a minimal rest but ready to do our job. Heading out of Salt Lake City was another chore. We were delayed due to an unexpected government entourage. The Captain notified me we were twenty-two on the list for a take-off. *Rats!*

"Does anyone want to sing 'America the Beautiful' as we wait for our take-off?"

Only the folks from Montana can make the best of another test of patience. Arriving back to Salt Lake City from Billings, Montana, we were now headed to Fargo, North Dakota. Switching from one aircraft carrier to another can be a mind-boggling effort. Thank goodness, we utilize one another's brain cells for where we are, what time zone we're in, and what flight we are operating for Angel Air. It becomes a conflicting schedule. The grueling part of this job is a weakened night's rest, for we're always dealing with constant alterations.

Departing the next day to finalize our four-day trip is always a grace. Arriving into Denver, I prepared the cabin for a final descent. We had to do Fargo, Denver; Grand Junction, Colorado; and back to Denver. We get excited knowing we are on a final stretch. Suddenly, I heard an alarm signal going off in the flight deck. Captain Aaron informed me we missed our approach to the runway due to a congested landing area. Therefore, a turnaround was crucial. I could feel the aircraft going from a descent to an immediate climb in a jiffy.

Not to alarm the passengers is a must, yet this gravitational pull made every passenger's stomach spin like a broken Ferris wheel. I prayed in my jump seat for our safety.

When I felt a tilt in an upward motion, I knew there was a problem. We had an aircraft underneath with no signal to alert us, yet despite a blind spot for our First Officer, she managed to tackle the problem with incredible ability and performance. Upon landing in Denver, we made a safe arrival due to my fellow workers addressing this situation with much stability and accuracy. I salute my fellow team members for not stressing out in a moment of potential crisis, although I felt in my heart and soul we were contending with an unstable situation. Our professional training with Angel Airlines is an advantage. It made me confident as a Flight Attendant, knowing we are a team working together for the sake of our passengers. It can be a rough go out there, yet we seem to keep the spirit flowing. Know you have an extraordinary family within this business. We are bonded and skilled at our job, through thick and thin.

Going in Circles

ONCE AGAIN, I'M NEVER SURPRISED AT THE in-flight occasion. Captain Troy and I were the only consistent flight crew through the duration of our trip series in August. We went through five First Officers due to crew scheduling procedures. We entailed many storms after returning home from Great Falls, Montana. Troy attempted to land the aircraft, although we were diverted to Colorado Springs, Colorado, due to Denver, Colorado, closing down. We circled for some time above Denver to get a chance at landing. It didn't happen. Therefore, we were on our way to an undisturbed airport in Colorado Springs. It looked like a class reunion with many jets stuck. Many planes lined up waiting for Denver to reopen. We had a few passengers onboard whose final destination was Colorado Springs. They wanted to deplane. Captain Troy got their bags from the bin from the help of First Officer Dustin lifting his fanny into the cargo area. How I laughed at this scene. Unfortunately, we were in breach of security, trying to assist passengers to get to their destination in a time of need. Shame on us! We were only trying to assist our customers, but we have to play by the rules. The storms eventually cleared out of Denver, and we were on our way. Arriving to the gate was a total mob lynching. I needed another fire extinguisher to put out the unbelievable impact of passengers needing to get to Tulsa after such heavy delays. It resembled a Denver Bronco football game losing in the last few minutes of the ball game. We ended up landing into

Tulsa over three hours late. Our crew was pooped. We had an early showtime the next day but delayed it for an hour so we could rest in Tulsa, Oklahoma.

Getting up in the morning hours, we dealt with much heat and humidity. My nylons were already soaked from humidity as we climbed into the van for our route to the Tulsa airport. Rachel kicked into gear as our First Officer back to Denver. She was terrific through the storms. Arriving into Denver, we now have another First Officer by the name of Jim. He used to be in law enforcement and shared many of his officer stories with us. We were in dire need of food, for we had not eaten a decent meal in several hours. Arriving into El Paso, Texas, we wanted some good Mexican food. We ended up at Chile's restaurant. Food is a necessity to regain our strength. Coming back to the hotel, I went to the pool to relax while the guys took a snooze. We all needed to unwind.

We departed the next day back to Denver. We had another First Officer by the name of Matt. There were more problems on the ground due to a misfit printer and an aborted take-off trying to get to Winnipeg, Canada. I knew there was an error once I felt a lack of surge on take-off. Troy contacted me to keep me abreast of the situation. We returned to the gate to fix the troubles. Once again I had to entertain passengers onboard due to our delay and unruffle many nervous reactions. It seems natural to turn on a positive light, for it eases the turmoil. They were amazed at my input to diligently handle another misfortunate incident within the airline industry. I was asked if I ever thought of going on a comedian's show. Wouldn't that be a keen idea? The world is too stressed right now. Sharing a smile is a random act of kindness and seemingly medicating in situations like this. Anger, anxiety, and lashing out are not a solution to inflict on one another, especially in this business. Humor and determination is our coping tool. My genetic makeup must be one huge endorphin.

Upon our arrival into Winnipeg, Canada, we were limp without a meal. We checked into our hotel and proceeded to locate some grub. Entering into a small restaurant, we got the stare down. They knew we weren't locals. Chewing tobacco, while sipping on suds and dipping fries into brown gravy, we decided to locate a different dining establishment. This was Captain Troy's 35th birthday and we wanted him to have a special memory. We located a nice place on top of a roof to overlook this fantastic city. It was wonderful. Coming back to our hotel we entailed an underground mission. We spun in circles, attempting to cross the street to our hotel. It led us back to the initial entry point. We were confused with which direction we were going. It was a labyrinth under the street much like being trapped in a mouse maze. It left us in a quandary of being guided in a hidden tunnel under the earth. By playing "Follow the Leader" we managed to devise a way out!

Returning to Chicago, Illinois; Lincoln, Nebraska; Denver, Colorado; Colorado Springs, Colorado; and back to Denver was a precarious trip. We had many storms once again to deal with, although my in-flight friends made this trip an unimaginable experience. It was a rough one due to turbulence, storms, and delays, but my travel time with five different First Officers made me wonder at the fuzzy math in the airline business. Captain Troy and I were a consistent twosome, appeasing any situation due to amusement and lessening conflicts of woe. Thank your fellow crewmates. It can be an extraordinary asset in life!

Ma, Pa, and Son

LEAVING DENVER, COLORADO, FOR GREAT FALLS, MONTANA, and Fayetteville, Arkansas, in August, First Officer Ryan and I met at gate 58 for introductions. We had a sudden gate change to 54. Loading up our gear, we made the transfer. Then we were notified the departure was going to take place out of gate 60. It felt like we were in the movie *Airplane*, with passengers following us from one gate to another. Ryan and I did our preflight, waiting for Captain Aaron. We waited for forty-five minutes. I knew he was present because I had lunch with him earlier in our crew lounge. However, the boards displaying flight information were malfunctioning, causing much confusion for everyone. By a whim, Aaron stumbled onto our aircraft, looking for us. This was a hide-and-go-seek crew member game with many gate changes. Tag . . . the Captain was it. We apologized to our passengers. Finally, we were on our merry way to our destinations, making up for lost time.

Our overnight was in Fayetteville, Arkansas, where the humidity had all of us breaking a sweat at 10:00 p.m. Even though the air-conditioning was working, the high density of humid air was seeping into my room through the cracks. It felt like I had four hours of rest, as my wake-up call came too soon. This is typical with early showtimes. We arrived in Chicago, Illinois, grabbed a bite, and sat in the crew lounge, listening to many weather stories and delays.

Fortunately, we departed from Chicago to Winnipeg, Canada, where it was nice and cool with a sixty-five-degree temperature. I took a hike near Red River and spotted a riverboat ship. I will have to try that next time, I thought. In the meantime, I enjoyed the rapture of a flowing river and mild temperatures. Returning to the hotel, the three of us took off for Bleachers, a local sports pub nearby. We met the owner, who grilled us a good-sized hamburger piled high with fries. Sitting in a booth, a Canadian by the name of Kerri asked if he could join us.

We looked at one another, exchanging glances, then uttered, "Sure, why not?"

Kerri was a local chef extremely inquisitive and very interested in American politics. He drilled us with questions regarding our economy, health-care programs, government, and environmental issues in the USA. It felt like we were being screened for a CNN special report. Aaron and Ryan had an answer for every question he fired at them.

Feeling adequate with the answers he received, Kerri bade us farewell, replying, "Not only is your son friendly, Leenda, he's also intelligent, eh."

Captain Aaron looked at me, muttering under his breath, "Hey, Ma, would you like to get to know Pa better and have a hot date tonight?"

We all howled over this "Ma, Pa, and Son" scene, for we were simply crew members for Angel Air and this man had no clue. Do we look like a nomadic family? With as much as we're on the road together, the answer to that question is, probably so. How can a Captain and Flight Attendant with blond hair and light eyes produce a son with dark hair and brown eyes? Just another token of comedy.

Leaving the next morning, we passed through two major storm cells. It was a tricky ordeal, but Pa and Son made Ma proud of a safe landing. Stopping in at Denver, we got our coffee fix at Starbucks. This was enough to keep our engines going. Leaving for Bismarck, North Dakota, was a smooth sail, thank goodness. We waited forty-five minutes for the van to pick us up, but kept the jokes going. Welcome back to another dose of heat and humidity. We wrapped up our trip with a Ground Round burger on our frugal budget, but sharing more patriotic quests in the sky as a family was a highlight.

Crews Can Cruise

BOARDING THE TRAIN IN DENVER, COLORADO, I have learned to become a gal on the move. Departing concourse B, I was executing an effort to catch my regional bus, or else I would be delayed for another hour. The adrenaline our crew members maintain upon conclusion of any trip is phenomenal. We're more aggressive than an NFL defensive football team with our black bags on wheels, ready to knock over any passenger in our pathway. Our professional nature clocks out the minute after we've completed a trip series. If you think you want to get to your destination, the only thing we desire as crew members is to arrive at our doorstep in one piece, with some degree of sanity. Most important is, we want to go home. We deal with time zone changes, stiff pillows and beds, leaking toilets, wicked weather patterns, mechanical problems, and dining on morsels for breakfast, lunch, and dinner. It's time to go home.

We turn into human bullets, trying not to injure nor maim—although stand to the side when you witness a white shirt with stripes, pilot's cap, bomber jacket, or navy-blue polyester uniform dashing through.

Racing through the concourse, I leaped on the escalator. I heard the train arriving. *Bam, bam, bam,* down the steps clanged my crew bags as I attempted to hop on. I barely made it as the door was closing, giving the ugly warning signal with a message: "You are delaying the departure of this train." So much for the guilt factor.

An Asian passenger on the train exclaimed, "You looked like a ballerina coming into the train."

I acknowledged, "No, sir, I believe I resemble a baseball player sliding into home plate or a football player running for a touchdown!"

Coming into concourse A, I observed a Captain from Frontier Airlines attacking the same action I just completed. Another *bam, bam, bam* affair with crew bags flitting down the escalator. I think I'd call this baggage abuse, but we don't care at this point. He barely made it before the door closed while skidding onto the train. We gave one another a high-five, knowing we were done with our trip assignment. I asked him if he just finished a four-day trip series. He nodded yes.

A passenger on the train inquired, "Do we have to pay for this entertainment, or is this free of charge?"

I responded, "It's free of charge, but a lesson to learn is never get in the way of a crew member. We are bulldozers to get to our plane on time or when we're through with our trip series. Our shoes can jaunt into a rapid pace."

Everyone on the train applauded my reply and gave us a nod. They wished us well and informed us to keep up the great work ethic. If passengers think they are discouraged due to delays, so are crew members. We miss our own comfy beds, homemade meals, family, and friends too. We sympathize with the discouraging moments of being removed from a home environment. Our energy is on a high alert as we attempt to catch the employee bus, connecting flight, or other transportation to arrive home. A message of warning: **Be on guard when you see us coming.** We have the capacity to run at a quick pace, dragging our many bags behind us on wheels. Our intention is not to run over passengers, but we're just as excited as our travelers to get to a resting spot we like to call home. Red Rover, Red Rover, send a crew member right over.

Windy Blow

I HAD TO UNDERGO ANOTHER INTENSE TIME of air travel with my fellow crew members through the month of August. Going in and out of Montana can raise the stress level with unbelievable turbulence. This is pretty typical in this vicinity but was a new twist for me traveling over this area. I had an unimaginable incident while attempting to finish my duties on our aircraft. Trying to gather trash on the descent into Billings, Montana, I was tossed to and fro, banging my head on the overhead bins, attempting to get back to my jump seat. I fell on an empty seat. It was not the most feminine approach, with my heels dangling upside down in a vacant seat—although I was one determined lady, trying to get to a place of safety.

A kind man helped me regain my mobility. "Are you OK, my dear?" he asked.

"I'm just trying to get to my seat, sir," I responded.

When we finally landed in Billings on a safe mode, a passenger quizzed me regarding who helped me during my time of distress.

I informed him, "No."

He told me, "Well, Leenda, you almost landed in the lap of the governor in Montana. He probably enjoyed the memorable female move onboard."

My spontaneous reply was, "If I lived in Montana, he'd get my vote for being a caring individual with my embarrassing goal of getting to my jump seat in one piece."

This is just another example of "good news" as a Flight Attendant for Angel Air. I can't keep up with who's who on my flights, as passengers all blend into one massive blur traveling from one destination to another in our repeated travels. It's a relief we entailed a firm landing due to the incredible winds there.

Another place with high winds and constant precaution is the State of Wyoming. Upon landing into Cody, during our descent, I was hanging onto my beverage cart for dear life. It almost tipped on top of me as I raced through my service.

A passenger exclaimed, "Hey, Leenda, do you know why the winds are so bad in Wyoming?"

Trying to scramble back to my jump seat and secure the forward galley, I made a quick conversation with him.

"No, sir, I don't," I answered.

He advised me, "It's because many angels' wings from above are going up and down over our State of Wyoming."

Oh dear. If that's the case, then God, send more angels for protection, as I am worn out mentally and physically right now, trying to stand erect in the main cabin aisle.

Another tough area is traveling from Denver, Colorado, into Colorado Springs, Colorado. A quick fifteen- to twenty-minute flight can make me shiver in my jump seat from wind shear, low altitude, and one bouncy flight, thanks to the Rocky Mountains. I had a group with their hands up in the air like we were in Disneyland on the Matterhorn, thinking they were on a fun roller coaster ride. I must admit: it certainly felt like a nasty quick jaunt in my behalf, although the kids and their parents seemed to enjoy the event. I sure hope so, as my face turns green when engaging in these rapid trips.

Once again, it's a celebration for all crew members to know our passengers arrived home due to our strategy and steady communication. Whether it be a governor, an official member of the USA government, military personnel, law enforcement, pop rock band, or a simple grandparent visiting his or her loved one, it's all the same in my book of travels. They have a destination to arrive at in a safe and sound means, and we are here to assure that will transpire. Unfortunately, when we contend with turbulence, it's as hard on our nerves as it is on our passengers. The job as a Flight Attendant holds many responsibilities. I can rise to a cause when I hear many needs for the sake of the "flock." When in trouble, I simply submit a quiet prayer and ask for the Good Lord's help to guide this aircraft. He always hears a simple prayer. It's the ticket in life to tackle while in the sky.

Tag Team

HEADING ON ASSIGNMENT TO EDMONTON AND CALGARY, Canada; San Francisco, California; Orange County, California; and Eugene, Oregon, in August, was another trip to write about. Usually, I'm the only Flight Attendant onboard while working smaller aircrafts, but this trip required two, for it was a larger jet. I had the delight of being with my fellow Flight Attendant, Karim. We were a tag team onboard, giggling nonstop from the time we first met at the gate in Denver. She was Nurse Ratched, making sure passengers had their bags stowed properly in first class. Meanwhile, I was her sidekick in the main cabin. Our amusement was constant due to our many years of service within the airline industry. She was a former ramp agent like myself. We were quite skilled on what belongs onboard and what is unwilling to fit, no matter how hard our passengers jammed baggage into the overhead bins. We knew how to take care of business in getting an aircraft out on time, contending with the mess of oversize bags and special needs. Dealing with an aircraft on route to San Francisco with half of the aircraft not speaking English was certainly a special effort. We practiced patience and could've used an interpreter with many odd requests. We had to inform them that their snack was merely pretzels for the duration of the flight. Our Asian passengers were a joy to be with, even though our communication skills were a barrier. Regardless, using hand signals for a game of charades seemed to work.

Captain Wayne and First Officer Andrew loved joining the fun with their "gabby gals." Although it was a long journey going in and out of customs in Canada, we continued to fling jokes from every angle of the airport as we proceeded through the gates of our North American comrades. My duty was browsing the area for an affordable meal and beverages. I hiked the turf, checking out menus and prices to fit our airline budget. I have a pretty good "snoot" when it comes to locating bargains we can afford while on assignment. A block away from the hotel, Tony Roma's had a sale going on. I contacted the Captain when I arrived back to the room. We were gone in minutes to absorb this special time of bargain beverages and appetizers. Not only was this a fabulous deal but a delicacy!

Leaving once again in the early hours of the morning, trudging through the airport engaging customs, stripping to the bare necessities with security, we dropped our baggage and lunch pails in the dark as we stumbled through the aircraft to conduct our security search. Karim and I chuckled about our lifestyle as in-flight crew members. Our undertaking to arrive to an airport on time is essential. We have much to accomplish with paperwork, security checks, and in-flight responsibilities—especially when conducting an international flight before passengers hop onboard. Our eyeballs are still attempting to get into focus, but our bodies have already gone through an aerobic workout with replacing seat cushions; checking seat pockets, overhead bins, galley compartments, lavatory checks; and processing paperwork.

From the initial boarding process and for the remainder of the flight, we assist, listen, and provide our passengers with a unique service. An added advantage is when you can display together a workable team. This is a magnetic image when you're linked with a special in-flight friend. I had many passengers inquire if we were sisters. I pondered on this notion and replied, "Yes, she's my twin sista, all right!" I suppose both of us were destined on this trip sequence to create a wonderful memory for the sake of our customers. We cradled them to rest in a seat of comfort on a memorable Angel Air flight. No more can be said for God's talented "gabby gals."

Another token of grace is allowing your inner sun to shine on a few shaded areas in life. We have the capacity to be creative, yet our lighthearted mannerisms put everything into perspective with life in the sky. I understand we're always running from hub to hub. Our time clocks are overwhelming, although our wild and offbeat sense of humor carries us through the route. It's a necessary ingredient to maintain this erratic lifestyle we've all chosen.

Aye Yi Yi

CAPTAIN EDGAR, FIRST OFFICER LUKE, FELLOW FLIGHT Attendant Chandra, and myself were in San Antonio, Texas, in September 2008. Despite the unbearable heat, we managed to do the tourist thing. The van driver dropped us off at the River Walk. This is a popular area filled with restaurants, gift shops, historical buildings, vibrant paintings, and scenic statues. Taking the trolley to Market Street, we dined at a tasty Mexican restaurant. Little did we know, our Captain spoke fluent Spanish as we attempted to communicate with our server pointing to numbers on the food menu. As we joyfully sat there together, we were serenaded by a Mariachi band, which created a warm atmosphere of food, fun, and frolic. Edgar disclosed that he was born and raised in Mexico City. No wonder we looked so stupid trying to communicate in Spanish, but he enjoyed the ability to communicate in our behalf. We managed to pull off a "Si," yet we allowed him to do the rest of the conversation, for we were lost. Edgar is an informative Captain, filled with a load of information regarding his upbringing in Mexico City. I was in awe at his many teachings and learned much on this short trip series. Afterward, we ventured to the Alamo. The museum was a collection of artifacts describing the war between the United States and Mexico. Gazing at a miniature display of toy warriors and soldiers, it was obvious they were not prepared for this onslaught. I told Edgar this resembled the employees at an airport, overwhelmed with disgruntled passengers due to oversold flights. He giggled at my comment and added an, "Ai Yi Yi!" Edgar filled my noggin with historical information, for I had no previous knowledge of this revolution. Possibly, I skipped out on this portion of my history class in high school, but Edgar revived my brain cells. The grounds were well preserved with flourishing gardens. It was a fantastic sight. We took pictures and posed by the front doors of the Alamo. Luke and Chandra made a rustic move to pretend we were back in those days for a quick flick.

We had one more venture we wanted to accomplish before we left. It was time for a boat ride on the river, which flows throughout the vicinity at River Walk. Feeling like little children at Disneyland, we waved at tourists sitting outside on the patio. They cheerfully returned the same gesture. There was a marriage ceremony outside the River Walk, which added to our enjoyment, even though a few guys taunted, "You'll be sorry." It made all of us laugh. The sweet smell of flowers and scent of Mexican food flowing from restaurants was an inviting experience. San Antonio is a delightful city filled with festive, robust entertainment and fine dining. It's certainly an "Ai Yi Yi" place to visit. Just make sure you have an Edgar with you to explain the historical event of this city. It's an amazing tale.

My Happy Space

ARRIVING AT THE AIRPORT, I MET CAPTAIN Len and First Officer Keith. Already, the setting was flowing with humor. I could sense this was another terrific trio in the air. We operated a turn to Fargo, North Dakota, then headed to Kalispell, Montana. I slept like a newborn babe at the hotel. In the morning, I took a quick hike. It was attractive with the October hues and the changing leaves—such a refreshing change from the hustle and bustle at bigger cities and airports we visit. A slower pace certainly stimulates the soul. Heading back to my hotel room, it was time to pack my hiking boots and replace them with my Flight Attendant heels.

We ventured back to Denver, Colorado, in the afternoon, then were scheduled for Bakersfield, California, the same day. There wasn't much time in California except to rest for the next day; however, the sway of palm trees in the breeze was invigorating. The next day we flew to Salt Lake City, Utah. Time to play the ole switcheroo from one airline to another as we contract out with different mainline carriers that we work under. I have so many Post-It notes to remind me, not only where our destination is, but altering time changes and which carrier we're operating is a life preserver! It helps to have two more brains traveling with me in case I have a senior moment.

We were off to Tulsa, Oklahoma, on a sunny October morning. The flight was smooth as silk while performing my service. Halfway across Oklahoma, we encountered some clear air disturbance, which rocked the aircraft. The noise and sudden jolt created an off-balance situation, throwing me at an awkward angle from a standing position.

A passenger screamed out loud, "Something broke, or the bottom just fell of this here plane. Y'all better take cover!"

This caused widespread pandemonium onboard. I scurried backward with my beverage cart to the galley and restored it in its proper place. I never thought this ole gal's wheels could move so quickly in a reverse motion, but you rise to the cause and have to react in an immediate fashion. Captain Len calmly reported to our passengers what just transpired to settle their frayed nerves as well as mine.

Naturally, our well-trained pilots took care of business, to restore a safe flight. Arriving safely into Tulsa, Oklahoma, Len and Keith explained the impact of mountain wave activity and stagnant air pockets. Maybe our pilots don't understand human behavior, but as a Flight Attendant maybe I learned a valuable lesson with what our pilots deal with in flying an aircraft. Just another team effort in coaching, listening, and learning from one another.

The next day we headed to Chicago, Illinois. Seeking out the food court, we had a quick nibble in the concourse. We shared stories about our past airline experience and our childhood days. Len and I had a similar background, both attending Catholic grade and high schools—he, in San Diego, and myself, in Omaha. I shared with Len and Keith a story regarding our high school dances. At the time, the nuns used to chaperone our sock-hops. This was when slow dancing became a hot item. The sisters didn't appreciate the close contact and therefore would come up and remind us to make room for the Holy Spirit. I thought Len was going to choke on his chicken burrito while listening to my story. He shared his episodes serving as an altar boy. Keith suggested that the two of us needed to be separated due to our nonstop giggles growing up.

Over the years, my friends and I have invented an invisible square around what I call and consider my "happy space." It is where no person can enter nor disrupt. This is mine to keep and treasure. I've started a new club with my crew member friends in Denver and taught them how to discover the secret to happiness in life, which is to retain a "happy space." We are faithful siblings who understand a specific code within the in-flight business. It's our silent message to let one another know, "Life is good, I'm OK, and so is my trip series," while spotting one another across the tarmac, concourse, or swapping aircraft in different cities. Call it another silly plug in the airline industry, but it's a spontaneous action to share a unique bond of faith, hope, and love. In my Irish eyes, it's a special gift to share with others to acknowledge we're all in this together. Now that's a comforting thought to keep my "happy space" flowing.

Stranded in Aspen

OUR ATTEMPT TO MAKE IT OUT OF Aspen, Colorado, the weekend before Christmas 2007 was a gallant effort. A total of twelve crew members based out of Denver, Colorado, became stranded due to the harsh weather conditions. Traveling back and forth from the hotel to the airport felt like a boomerang. Our exertion to continue our flight trip series was terminated due to limited visibility, low ceiling, and a contaminated tarmac with breaking action at zero.

After spending many hours at the airport, we came to the conclusion that this was going to end up as a canceled flight. We decided to make the best of the moment by taking pictures at the airport's baggage claim area and outside, grasping snowflakes, like Lucy, with our tongues. We were a chipper group of children romping through the snowdrifts, creating makeshift snowshoes with thank-you bags to keep our toes warm through the raging snowstorm.

The van driver from our hotel took a group of us into town. Our decision to dine at Little Annie's overwhelmed the hostess with our invasion to eat. After waiting patiently to be seated, a server finally managed to greet us in a cheerful tone to promote the specials of the day. The cheapest thing was a filet mignon for $35.95. Ouch, that's not in our airline budget! Captain Craig found a popcorn machine and loaded us up with baskets of free popcorn on our tables as an appetizer. Some ordered food, while others munched on popcorn. It wasn't our intention to be a "scrooge" in Aspen, but most of us were on a tight budget—especially with holiday gifts for our families and friends. Not wanting to leave a minor currency token in our server's apron pocket, we tipped her well and wished the staff a happy holiday season. The hotel van picked us up at 10:00 p.m. to bring us back to our rooms. We sang Christmas carols and even invented a few of our own "12 Days of Christmas" with an Angel Air version. I don't know if our fellow hotel guests in the van appreciated our high spirits, but we remained festive despite a rough holiday attempt of trying to get back to Denver. This was yet another remarkable event in sharing a special moment with my in-flight friends. If this was a test to scrutinize our capacity for turning an unpleasant event into a joyous occasion, we certainly passed with flying colors. We never allowed our holiday spirit to dwindle. Just proof in the tapioca pudding, we can sing "Fa la la la la" despite any good, bad, or ugly situation.

Estrogen Express

TRAVELING FROM DENVER, COLORADO; GRAND JUNCTION, COLORADO; Wichita, Kansas, my trip series was a total female crew. Captain Barb, First Officer Lauren, Maria, and myself were ready to handle business. After a quick turn to Grand Junction, we were ready to board for Wichita. Many male senior citizens peeked into the flight deck.

To their amazement, they exclaimed, "Oh, no, it's women flying this darn airplane."

I speculated, *Hmm, how will I respond to this statement?*

I allowed my thoughts to fester a grand response. Clearing my throat, I replied, "Yes, sir, it's not your imagination. There are two women who will fly this aircraft to Kansas. By the way, even though they have ponytails and wear barrettes, remain at ease. They are still skilled pilots!"

Hearing this comment, my two pilots in the flight deck let out a burst of laughter. So did our female passengers boarding our plane. They chanted, "You're in the front seat for a change and are in charge. You go, gals!"

Even though a few male passengers were still procrastinating while arriving onboard, other lady passengers thought this was a great scene. Hang on, for this is your estrogen express flight, with a female crew. Sit back and relax, ladies and gentlemen. You're in excellent hands.

This was a smooth trip from Wichita into Denver. We landed with a wham, for that's Captain Barb's mark of a successful flight. We received a round of applause from our female passengers when we arrived on target. They showered us with jubilation and mentioned, "This was one fun flight." What a great feeling, as there is hesitation when some passengers view a female in the flight deck. Some assume a mode of narcissism. My question is, Do you think they could be retaining that seat in the flight deck if they had not passed their credentials in flight school or required FAA testing? Of course not. If you think women who steer the aircraft are incapable, it's time to re-calculate. I've been on many trips and trust my flight crews due to their experience and safety records whether male, female, young, or old. They have to attend a similar rigid training session, just as we Flight Attendants, every year. Captains have more responsibility required by the FAA. If you feel compelled to express an opinion on the reliability of our in-flight crew members, I suggest you twitter, tweak, or text someone who gives a hoot. We are well trained, thanks to our company, and proud of our efficiency to keep you updated with airline requirements. Be at peace, knowing we're doing our best to get you to your destination, provide a happy flight mode, and take care of your needs. Food for thought—if you undergo another all-women staff, maybe you should plant yourself on a seat, put on a sleep mask, and repeat, "There's no place like home . . . there's no place like home!"

All I can inform you is that this all-female team was an asset in my traveling background. We held tight together and proved we are certainly capable of pulling off a great trip series despite our hormones. To think we don't have the capacity due to our gender is a false reality. We are in-flight explorers decked out in polyester to serve you.

Muckluck

DEPARTING OUT OF DENVER, CAPTAIN CARSTEN, RESERVE First
Officer Tim, and I were in for another trembling undertaking. Flying
into Madison, Wisconsin, we encountered much turbulence due to
a thunderstorm on route. Lightning and heavy rain with swirling
winds made this one a nail-biter.

Gee, this is only March 2, and it's not even spring yet, I pondered.

We returned to Denver using a different route, but this was
a huge storm system. Of course, we had to swap aircrafts, entailed
weight and balance issues, and waited for our new First Officer coming in from Sacramento, California. I took bags off to place in the
bin underneath the aircraft but was informed by the Captain that I
needed to make room inside the cabin. A nonrevenue passenger was
given a seat then pulled off due to our weight restrictions. Another
passenger became rowdy. He was agitated with our delayed departure
to Wichita, Kansas. He ignited a match onboard to start a forest fire
of anger within the cabin. We were already experiencing problems,
but the heckler decided to make it worse. Steve landed at the oppo-
site end of the B concourse. He had to run a marathon to arrive at
our gate. In the meantime, this naughty passenger continued to voice
his sarcastic opinions to other passengers seated nearby. His boister-
ous round of applause when Steve made it was unnecessary. I was
contending with an obstinate human being. I checked the manifest
for this person's name. It was Muckluck. Now, that's an appropriate

name to sum up this day's event. I kept my cool but gave my pilots a heads-up regarding this passenger's behavior. He was teetering on crossing over a crew member's boundaries. I monitored his actions with a watchful eye.

Serving as a tour leader to several destinations in Europe and the USA, I've always inherited one stinker in the crowd attempting to ruin a person's travel experience. I'm quite aware of how to zero in on a situation before it escalates. This was my opportunity to zip his lips with my professional presence. I made passengers comfortable by offering water, pillows, and blankets until we departed.

He chimed in with a malicious comment, "Why don't you give the pilots a pillow, for they just sleep on the job anyway?"

The surrounding passengers were clearly becoming exasperated with his snide remarks. We finally departed for Kansas two hours late. Another annoying round of applause coming from his seat upon take-off.

"Hang in there, Leenda," I told myself.

It was time for the beverage cart and service with a smile, as always. I had to scurry, as this was a quick flight. Coming to his row with my cart, he demanded a free cocktail due to our late departure out of Denver.

I surprised him with a calm answer: "I'm so sorry, sir, for this inconvenience, but hopefully, this unfortunate experience won't become a sour grape in the near future with Angel Air."

Passengers surrounding him applauded my serene nature. You don't fight fire with fire. Best to kill this guy with tolerance, yet a warm-hearted attitude.

He had to include a final statement with, "I love you, Leenda."

My reply was, "Yep, I love you too, Mr. Man, but mind your manners."

When we arrived in Kansas, he thanked me for my capacity to turn a bad occurrence into a positive notion. He couldn't resist, when deplaning, to toss some foul language into the flight deck upon my fellow crew members. They were stunned. I had to inform them this was my penance onboard until we arrived. I managed to keep this one under my wing. Sure, he needed to be scolded, but I treated him like I would one of my kids. I have much patience, but don't cross my mom line. Many of my departing passengers gave me an embrace and told me what a great job I did in handling this incident. That's always a gratuity, for we are an earnest team working together to provide an enjoyable, professional, and safe travel encounters.

By the time we arrived in Wichita, it was cold and windy. Arriving to our hotel, we were worn out from the day. I meditated, *Isn't every day a Muckluck adventure?*

We were held up in Wichita due to heavy flow in Chicago, Illinois, the next day, so we went on a hotel tour with Trisha. She informed us this hotel is well preserved with a history of aviation, including Charles Lindbergh residing here during his travels. It also served as an underground gambling headquarters, brewery, and lots of ladies in the days of prohibition. Al Capone was another frequent visitor. No wonder we witnessed many underground tunnels and massive rooms underneath the hotel. This was quite a lesson. In addition, we learned that the hotel is also noted for its ghost tales. One is by the name of Clarence. It seems his spirit is still roaming the hallways. According to Trisha, many strange affairs have happened here and still continue to take place. We were told he likes certain crew members, and others, he pulls pranks on. Good thing we're on his favorable invisible side. This tops off our debut in Kansas. It's time to fly and say bye-bye. I think we've had our fill of *Ghostbusters* on the ground!

Leaving for Chicago the next day, I had another full load. Many senior citizens were traveling with us. I helped buckle up their seat belts, tie their shoes, and guide them to the restroom before we left Wichita. The poor little fragile ones hit my Flight Attendant button one too many times, for they couldn't see the proper buttons designating an overhead light. It was a senior citizen adventure all right. One husband was deeply disturbed with his wife. By mistake, she packed both sets of dentures into their checked bags; therefore, they couldn't dine on pretzels.

He protested, "By golly, if she had gotten her fanny going in the wee hours, I could've enjoyed a snack."

Astonished with his remark, I murmured, "Oh, calm down, Grandpa. Please leave Grandma alone. She did the best she could in packing up your gear. Make sure your choppers are in your carry-on bags. Now give her a kiss, say you're sorry, and the next time you travel, it's your turn to pack the bags."

Grandma gave me a thumbs-up with that statement!

After arriving into Chicago, we left for Sioux Falls, South Dakota, dealing with more turbulence. This was getting to be a long journey. We arrived late and needed to get to bed. No relaxation for the weary crew members. Our showtime was at 5:59 a.m. instead of 5:15 a.m. Best to enjoy every minute of slumber.

It was a short night, but we left Sioux Falls on route to Chicago. Arriving into Chicago, I was informed I needed to run a round trip to Traverse City, Michigan, and back, for they needed a Flight Attendant. The reserve flight crew from Chicago laughed, for I walked like a Popsicle from one aircraft to another. Up, up, and away over a frigid Lake Michigan. Returning to Chicago, I was elated to be rejoined with my original flight buds even though I resembled a frozen ping-pong ball. I was delirious with time zones and cold winter conditions. A toasty beach with palm trees swaying in the wind is more my style. I had to keep dreaming, for this winter's clutch had left us with many frozen limbs thus far. Now we were headed to Winnipeg, Canada. Better break out my winter woolies for the North Pole. My buds and I headed to *Bleachers* for some grits. I convinced everyone to visit this local sports establishment, for they prepared one great burger. It warmed you up to tolerate the harsh sting of bitter, cold temperatures.

Departing Winnipeg to Denver the next day, we're ready to end this four-day trip series. I had a lady ready to throw up in the cabin, another worried about their connection in Denver, and crying babies onboard. I felt like joining the tots, as I needed a "whining" time-out myself. Yes, this was a Muckluck trip to remember. It is pretty remarkable what we can entail in only four days. Hurray to my fellow crew members. We do survive many unusual components, but we rise to the plate despite the unforeseen problems. May we continue to stick together like Elmer's Glue. Now it's time for a hot bath at home to thaw out my body.

March Expedition

LEAVING DENVER WITH MY FRIENDS CAPTAIN RICH and First Officer Auggie, nothing was going right. Our APU was in-op; mechanical problems with exit lights needed to be repaired before take-off; and dealing with disgusted passengers was the start of our four-day trip together. Auggie's Latin American accent seemed to woo our passengers with his in-flight announcement for take-off. I handed out bottled water to calm down our upset passengers. We finally took off and landed into Burbank, California. Auggie's announcement of waiting for "rump employees" to marshal us into the gate area, created a few snickers.

What a great deal to bask in some warm sunshine after many travels to the northern tundra dealing with below freezing temps. We headed to San Francisco, California, afterward. I had a passenger by the name of Winnie terrified to fly. It was on my manifest. My daughter and sister have a fear of flying. Therefore, I was prepared with the same behavior problems I have dealt with before. Boy, was I wrong. This gal went into a total panic attack after I placed her in a bulkhead seat. Her body almost went into a seizure due to anxiety from Burbank to San Francisco. As she curled over like a Cheetos, curled up in her seat, I had to rub her back and calm her fears to prevent her from losing oxygen.

I replied, "Winnie, it's OK, it's OK," in a low soothing voice, like a mom singing a melody to her newborn baby.

She was blowing in a sick bag to retain oxygen. Gazing up at me, she responded with a, "Woof, woof, woof, I'm doing just great."

I'll be darned, as this appeared to be a distraught passenger in my book of training, and I was ready to don my portable oxygen bottle. I continued to sit by her side to calm her down as her body was shaking so bad; she had no control over her sensitivity.

A passenger behind her questioned, "What the heck is going on, Leenda?"

I informed my frequent flyer, "She's scared to fly, sir."

He shook his head and claimed, "I do this flight every week, and it's safer than driving a car on the California highway."

Well, congrats for your input, although there are people with true fears onboard. I've dealt with passengers in their fear of flying in the past, but this one took the trophy. Getting Winnie to San Francisco in one piece was an exuberant and draining mission. I was pretty worn out by the time we arrived, but she made it through the flight. She gave me a hug of thanksgiving. I informed her that she may need to contact a physician the next time she travels. Anti-anxiety drugs work wonders these days for people with a significant fear of flying.

We traveled back to Burbank to overnight. Getting ready to have some fine dining, I spotted my old roommate, Natalie, from initial Flight Attendant training who is still based in Salt Lake City. I had not seen her since our training days. What a treat. We ventured for some pizza at a nearby restaurant. I then left the young pups behind as I needed some sleep. My plan was to hit the pool in the morning.

I woke up early to read my *USA Today*, sip on a hot cup of java, and nestle in the warm rays by the pool. This radiant glowing star of a sun is indeed a wonderful gift—along with palm trees, flowers, and green grass—after dealing with much cold weather during my travels. My buds joined me poolside after they woke up. We poked fun at one another due to our beaming white legs and no shade of brown on our bodies. I performed a few synchronized swim moments for my fellow crew members to engage in. Auggie will never make the Olympic team. That's for sure. It was time to don our uniforms and become a professional staff once again. Oh, this is difficult to leave sunny California and venture into Wisconsin. From a swimsuit to sweats is typical of a flight crew member. Not only do we adjust to many time zones, our bodies deal with many weather changes. No wonder we keep vitamin C handy.

Arriving into Milwaukee, Wisconsin, we were in for a switch of temperatures. It was cold, windy, and snowy. Our systems went into shock, knowing we were swimming in a pool a few hours ago. Winter's grasp is a dose of reality arriving into Wisconsin. It's still winter, regardless of the precious memories by the pool. All of us received a slight sunburn in Burbank. Now we were getting blasted by a whiteout blizzard while crossing the tarmac to get inside the terminal. I heard a voice call out to me.

It was Auggie, yelling, "Leenda, Leenda, was it my imagination, or didn't we sit by a pool just a few hours ago?"

I answered him in my distress, "No, Auggie, it was only a temporary moment of paradise. I hope you treasured the occasion."

I heard him blurt out an explosive laugh, although I couldn't see him nor Rich as we plunged through the snowdrifts. We hustled to our hotel room, dealing with daylight saving time's along with differing time zones. We were all out of whack. All of us got some much-needed sleep.

Attempting to grab a bite at the hotel, we got an opportunity to chat and share stories. Auggie saw a picture of my daughter.

He immediately retorted, "I'm in love, I'm in love, Leenda. You could be my future "mum-in-law.""

I instructed him, "If you mess with her, I'll hang you with a noose off a jet bridge in Denver, pal. I have many buds in the Colorado law enforcement who will monitor your South American charisma."

He simply chuckled. Just another kid I've taken under my wing for protection. I feel his spirit is free-flowing like mine. Being far from his homeland has been a hardship. He misses his family in Argentina, especially his "Mum." I can't say I blame him. It is no wonder that we take care of one another when there's a missing component. We become a surrogate family, watching over one another in this industry, providing and caring for one another's needs. Captain Rich joined in on the conversation with much feedback due to our travels. We bade one another a good night and hit the sack in our hotel rooms with a sunburn from Burbank and ready to toss our bodies in the nearest snowdrift to cool the pain in Milwaukee.

We left the next day to Fayetteville, Arkansas, home of Walmart headquarters. We may spend time in Fayetteville at our hotel room near the airport, but their hospitality is worth the weight in gold. They are very accommodating with their Southern accents. It's a day of staying fit as a fiddle in the workout room to remove the "blubs" from snacking on too many lunch pail snacks. We try to keep fit, but sometimes the fatigue we entail is an overload. We managed to make it back to Denver in one piece the next day.

Auggie yelled across concourse B, "Bye, Leenda, and take care of yourself."

My response was, "Back at you, my dear friend."

It's always a blessing to come home and unwind.

Bella

ON A FLIGHT SERIES, WHICH I HAD in March, was an Italian Captain
and German Irish First Officer for our trip to Burbank, California.
They spotted me in the gate with my Irish gear on, since I was not
going to be home for another Saint Patrick's Day celebration. We
entailed more turbulence on route due to high winds. Already, I felt
my shamrocks growing limp. We flew from Burbank, California,
to San Francisco, California, where I was spotted by a lead Flight
Attendant for compliance. I passed all the requirements; although
battling high winds on the tarmac, my hairdo looked like a bad corn
beef casserole. I was offered some Victoria's Secret gel from Judy to
fluff up my follicles. First Officer Adam got a charge out of that one.
We then left from San Francisco back to Burbank. I had a passenger
dealing with claustrophobia. It was only a forty-five-minute flight,
but for him, it was an eternity being seated in the back of the aircraft.
I moved him up front to be near my station. I informed the Captain
I may have a problem child but would monitor his behavior. With
my Irish wit, I concentrated on making him laugh. This resolved any
fear factor he was dealing with. Maybe my shamrocks were coming
alive once again. 'Tis the wearing of the green.

Burbank was gorgeous. I made a vow to hit the pool the next
morning to capture some sunshine before we had to leave for Denver,
Colorado, and Milwaukee, Wisconsin. Greeted with a *bella* remark
in the hotel lobby by our Captain, I needed to brush up on my Italian

and find out the meaning. It stands for "beautiful." I wonder why he never mentioned that yesterday when my hair was in a startled state. Oh, well! Once again we dealt with high winds returning to Denver then Milwaukee. The winds never seemed to ease up. Arriving into town, we darted for Houlihan's restaurant for one Irish toast before they shut down. My Irish ancestors would be so disappointed if I never had even a short and sweet celebration. Although there was no time for corn beef, cabbage, or Irish jigs, it was a hootenanny. The weather in Milwaukee was similar to Ireland, cold and rainy. All of us snoozed in the next day.

We went to work out in the gym in the morning and had lunch together. We then found out our inbound flight was delayed almost three hours. Therefore we retrieved our hotel cards and went back to our rooms. Sitting around a hotel room makes you want to go back to sleep. It's a dilemma while waiting on a clock with minimal rest and exhaustion. Here we sat in our rooms, eating more food out of our lunch pails and playing the waiting game. I wish they had a treadmill in my room to work off more calories consumed from the waiting process. I watched *Nanny McPhee* and the beginning of the miniseries *John Adams* until I heard from the fellas regarding our status.

Ultimately, we finally left for the airport at 6:20 p.m. for our Milwaukee-Chicago flight. Our Captain was busy handing out gum to appease the passengers. He played a great temporary Italian Easter bunny with his distribution of snacks. We blew in over two hours late and had to swap aircraft in Chicago for our next flight into Fayetteville, Arkansas, preflight and meet our new Captain, Ben. Here we went again with turbulence going boing-boing to Arkansas with thunderstorms. We had to circle due to winds at high knots.

Passengers were getting restless. I prayed for a safe landing. I think I wore out the heavens with my nonstop prayers. Sure enough, we started to descend. The wings rocked like a swing set, but our landing was on target due to gifted pilots. The van driver remarked that we were fortunate to make it in as this area was plagued with thunderstorms, floods, and tornadoes. It was only mid-March. Traveling from sweet sunshine in California to snow, sleet, cold, and wind in the Midwest, now entering into humidity, lightning, and thunderstorms in the South is an extreme. Oh, no, Dorothy, this is not Kansas, but Arkansas. Our passengers thanked us for getting them to their destination. We were worn out from the weather conditions. We're never aloof in our duties when it comes to safety—just a shackled bunch on an ominous flight path. Maybe my next trip series and hairdo will surpass a "bella" occasion.

Birthday Suit in Milwaukee

I GOT UP EARLY THIS MORNING TO enjoy a time-out by the pool in Burbank before we had to leave for Denver, Colorado, Milwaukee, Wisconsin, on our flight series. It was a lovely March day in sunny California. I enjoyed the moment, as the bitter winter had taken a pinch on the nerves of passengers and crew members.

Arriving at the hotel in Milwaukee, around 11:00 p.m., I was checking my e-mails with a group of young people in town for a sporting event. Suddenly, a young lady came racing around the corner in a panic, yelling there was a man running around the hallway with no clothes on.

"You've got to be kidding me," I said.

Hesitating, I went to inspect the situation. Sure enough, I spotted a man strolling down the first floor in the buff trying to put his key in the door but with no luck.

I approached the front desk and informed the head clerk some dude was hitting the hallways in his birthday suit. She followed closely behind me then spotted his pale cheeks. With no security available, she contacted the head bartender. The three of us kept the young people behind the scene as we approached this guest now hiding behind the vending machines for protection. Did he think a bag of chips would cover his loins?

The bartender addressed, "Sir, just what do you think you're doing, running around like this with no clothes on? You can't roam the hallways exposing yourself. We've got a reputation to maintain."

He managed to utter a meek whisper, "I'm locked out of my room."

Hearing this reply, the high school kids went into hysterics. One youth mentioned, "If this was Saint Patrick's Day, we could hand him a few shamrocks."

Now here is a young man with the same Irish thoughts as myself. The hotel staff handled the situation properly while providing the guest with another card and a towel. I was sure room 127 would be a topic of conversation among the athletes during the tournament the next day, but these young folks took it in stride.

I felt bad for what they were exposed to, but I'm sure they had perceived worse. As a parent, I was embarrassed for this man flashing himself with no remorse. Nothing seems to rattle my cage anymore, although this was a first in my hotel experiences. I'll continue to share positive values to young people with any opportunity to meet them in so many cities during my traveling times. Let's continue to give them a spark of encouragement. Being their elders, we have the capacity to redirect and inspire their future. They depend on us as role models, relying on wisdom and knowledge. The "good news" is, we can achieve this with our clothes on to capture their attention.

Hopefully, this incident wouldn't show up in their yearbook. I'd have a lot of explaining to do with my mug showing up on a page with a man in his birthday suit lurking in the background. Kids will be kids, yet they still exhibit an optimistic attitude as our future leaders. For inquiring minds who want to know, this was **not** a fellow crew member captured in the raw. We have more class.

I Ain't Skeered

TRAVELING WITH CAPTAIN ERIC AND FIRST OFFICER Pete, we were on a constant delay leaving Denver, Colorado, to Rockford, Illinois, for a quick one-leg trip on April 1. I met Pete at gate 93. He had a radiant smile and shook my hand with a vibrant grasp. Captain Eric appeared to be stressed, probably due to his commute from California. I can always sympathize with a commuter, for it can be a rough go to report for duty in a station away from your hometown. When passengers began the boarding process, I informed them their flight to Rock Springs, Wyoming, was going to be a full flight. The looks I received were ones of shock and dismay, thinking they boarded the wrong aircraft. It was simply a good old April Fools' joke for me to ease the tension due to their delay in Denver. They were all good sports to create a fun flight onboard. They even had a few paybacks for me during my service to call it even with April Fools' humor. Good thing we had some tailwinds behind us to Rockford, making up for our one-hour delay. Not only were we on time but fifteen minutes early. This is reason to rejoice since the airlines are under pressure with on-time performance.

Arriving at the hotel, we scrambled to get our keys. This hotel offers a theme room, which I find entertaining. Some of my fellow crew members I've been with in the past don't care for the glitz. I love it, for it sets a different tone from the same scene every week spending time in hotels. I received the Italian room, while Pete was in the Mediterranean, and Eric in the American Victoria. Pete and I met in the restaurant for a quick bite, laughed about several stories, then headed to bed. I rested well in the Italian room with visions of rigatoni dancing in my head.

The next day we were on route to the airport. The hotel was having transportation difficulties with their broken-down vans. We were escorted to the airport in a limo. The looks we received driving down the interstate were hilarious. Folks were stretching their necks to see who was in the limo. Maybe it's Jay Leno, Oprah, or possibly Billy Joel? No, it's just crew members slipping to the Rockford airport in style. When we arrived, the limo driver grabbed me and gave me a huge kiss good-bye. It caught me off guard, but my fellow crew members got a charge out of this farewell.

When we arrived, we found out our flight was running late from a mechanical problem in Denver. We sat, stared at the sights in the airport, and dug into our lunch pails. Two and a half hours later, our aircraft arrived. We scrambled onboard to preflight, got our paperwork resolved, and simultaneously boarded passengers. It's always a hard task to make up for lost time, but we try our best. People from the Midwest are very considerate of the hardships we undergo. Possibly my background of living in Nebraska most of my life taught me some easy rules to abide by. I know how to communicate with my fellow "corn friends." We have a common bond. It's called patience.

We returned to Denver with a short turn. Captain Eric grabbed me a cup of Starbucks to keep my momentum going. We shortly had to fly Cedar Rapids, Iowa, then off to Chicago, Illinois, circling for a landing, then placed in the "holding zone." I like to refer to this as the "aviation bull pen," waiting for a gate to open up. Our pilots did a superb job getting us back on track, although we still had to fly to Green Bay, Wisconsin. These pilots were on a mission, for we landed into Green Bay early. Cheers to my fellow crew members!

We met at Big D's restaurant in the hotel for some chow and refreshments. Eric proceeded to share a personal experience with us. He and his girlfriend entangled an ordeal a few years ago while visiting the Smoky Mountains. They hit an area of unforeseen territory and were met by a group of locals wondering what their intention was. One of the men posed a statement to Eric: "I ain't skeered." Being alone without any backup, Eric used much tranquility to escape from a possible bad situation of being outnumbered. At the time, he was shaking in his boots—although he remained confident to proceed with his travel plans while protecting his lady. We snickered over his ability to place many expressive comments with this story he shared with us. Little did I realize, it was a sentence I'd use over the next few traveling days.

We departed from Green Bay into Chicago, Illinois, the next day. This was an appropriate title for what we were about to undergo on route to Nashville, Tennessee, dealing with thunderstorms and tornadoes plaguing the East. A bolt of lightning under the aircraft lit up the cabin with our descent into Nashville. I almost needed to hand out Depend diapers onboard and save a few for myself in my jump seat. It was a flip-flop event. I kept reflecting on Eric's words the night before. It helped me get through this terrible storm and keep passengers calm. Coming from different backgrounds or raised in other states, crew members share a unique lifestyle together on the road. Our words warrant a time of understanding, encouragement, and brush of laughter. It's a valuable treasure onboard to remind fellow crew members of Eric's famous words of wisdom . . .

"I ain't skeered."

Harbor Time

DUE TO AN APRIL SPRING STORM, WE were delayed in and out of Denver. Our trip on day 1 consisted of Denver, Colorado; Colorado Springs, Colorado; Nashville, Tennessee. I met my fellow Flight Attendant, Lee, at gate 60. Our gate was switched to 56 as we played another hide-and-go-seek game as crew members. We were delayed two and a half hours to Colorado Springs, Colorado. Josh was our temporary Captain and Jen, our First Officer. Returning to Denver, we picked up Captain Steve. He was fortunate not to entail this quick turn, as he commutes from California. Another tribulation for commuters. At any rate, Lee and I hit it off from the start with our mom sense of humor. Here come the "golden girls." I was Maude, Lee was Blanche, and Jen was Rose. Poor Steve was outnumbered with this harem, but his jolly spirit kept on going. We arrived in Nashville with bad thunderstorms. We didn't need to visit Six Flags, for our job already provided us with a gravitational pull in the sky with a loop-the-loop affect. It was a short night of rest as usual, yet we needed to fly back to Denver early the next day then travel to Wichita, Kansas.

Denver was plagued with snow, sleet, and ice the following day, whereas Wichita was windy, cold, and rainy. Gads! Winter had worn out its welcome thus far. People were in dire need of a break with some sunshine. Steve, Lee, and I grabbed a bite to eat in the hotel restaurant. Little did we know, a local radio station was sponsoring a singles' party. We played a bingo game, observed a scavenger hunt, and I even won a door prize from a local Western country singer's CD. We joined in on the fun. Lee and I were single, but poor married Steve was getting attacked by quite a few Midwest gals on the prowl. He was a huge hit but retained a great sense of composure. His humble remark was, "Oh, I live in California and like to drive sports cars." That's all it took for the women to fall over him. Lee and I had to shield our Captain from their grip. My ribs hurt from laughing so hard due to this off-the-wall activity in Kansas.

Leaving the next day was an early showtime. We headed to Los Angeles, California, then to Vancouver, Canada. I was thrilled, for I've never been to this area before. Even though we were tired from our early-morning wake-up call, we got a second wind to discover a new city. Must be our adrenaline kicking in one more time. We took a city bus from our Delta Hotel to downtown Vancouver. Scooting through Stanley Park was impressive, especially since the cherry blossoms were in full bloom. What a pleasing sight. Jen was on a mission to see dolphin whales at the aquarium. The prices were relatively high with not much time to visit her whales. Yet Lee and I found another back road and an opportunity to view the animals before closing time. We were crew members, all right, lurking through the back door to capture the whales on our limited budget.

Afterward, we hiked many miles exploring this stunning area. We sat on a bench, like little children, observing Beaver and Otto seaplane tours departing the channel and arriving.

Steve sighed, "I wonder what my wife would say right now if she knew I was watching seaplanes with three women in Vancouver?"

Uttering a few praiseworthy comments from the ladies, we were once again a simple crew family absorbing the beauty of the Cascade Mountains in the background, observing an ocean wave weaving in and out of this channel, along with the scent of salt dotted with ships on the shore.

Getting back to our hotel was another classic event. We were told our bus back to the hotel was on another curb. We ran from place to place to catch our Canadian connection. Stupid us in trying to figure out where we're going in Canada. Due to intuition, we made it back in a quick means. Thank goodness. We had our jokes of whale droppings we observed on the shore, along with the clientele. This preserves and celebrates our faithful task while on the road together over a four-day span. No wonder I love being a part of this company. It's a living, but my fellow crew members keep me in a writing mode to share precious memories in life.

It's a Crew Thing

I TRAVELED WITH CAPTAIN RAMON, FIRST OFFICER Bryan, and Flight Attendant Tara in May of 2008. We split from Denver, Colorado, to Salt Lake, Utah; Los Angeles, California; Portland, Oregon. I was running on empty pockets with this schedule, but Tara kept me motivated. We did a quick turn from Portland to Los Angeles, back to Portland, then returned to Los Angeles the next day. It was a roundabout in the air. Finally landing in Los Angeles, it was great to get my toes on the ground. Tara wanted me to join in on the action in the city, touring a local mall near our hotel. Running low on finances due to being on a reserve status, I informed my crew that I was going to hit the sack and watch television.

She objected and remarked, "It's a crew thing for us to be together."

Even though my wages were depleted while waiting period for the next paycheck to deposit into my account, her lively spirit made me think twice. We took off on foot to discover the turf. We encountered a lost Caribbean–style restaurant filled with beach decor. We shared our in-flight stories and enjoyed some appetizers. Observing the California youngsters on skateboards, mopeds, and roller blades gliding through the mall area was stylish.

I mentioned to my friends, "Maybe we should invest in this equipment to get through airports."

On that note, I strolled back to the hotel, savoring the balmy temperatures. The rest of my crew decided to view more action in Los Angeles, although this lady was hitting the sack. My intention was to get up early, work out in the morning, and catch some rays near the pool.

It was a tad overcast the next day, for we wanted to hit the beach, but the pool was a nice treat. After my workout, I spotted my buddy Captain Len walking in the hallway with a few First Officers from Denver. I remarked, "Hey, this is an Angel Air reunion. Shall we meet in the pool to play Marco Polo?"

They shook their head at my suggestion and chuckled, for they were on their way to the airport. Yahoo, for I was on my way to the pool. I rocked out to my new Bee Gees CD, while Tara, Bryan, and Ramon enjoyed some sunlight. It was a little nippy to hop in the water although a rapturous time to be removed from the cold and snow, which continued to play havoc at our many destinations.

We left for Denver in the afternoon then onto Wichita, Kansas. After a good night's snooze in the so-called "haunted hotel," we hiked downtown to eat at a Mexican restaurant the following day. We also got a chance to tour the headquarters of an old castle built in downtown Wichita. It was remarkable to witness the traditions of this city. We dropped Captain Ramon off at the hotel while Tara, Bryan, and I continued our hike along the Arkansas River near our hotel. We received an education on the Prairie Indians, who established their roots here. It's a fascinating display of Indian history and a momentous tribute this city has to offer.

It was time to get back to our hotel room and get ready for our trip back to Denver. What a great time had by all. My special crew members made me redirect my actions and not ponder on my financial woes. Crew members have a silent formula. It's called friendship. It makes me appreciative of the effort we entail in taking care of one another. Having specific buds to travel with is a special perk. When Tara insisted this was a "crew thing," I understood her words of wisdom. Now, I pay it forward to others who are struggling like I was. Together we discover our destinations, whether we have a loaded checkbook or not. We're a troop in search of hidden valuables.

Airline Reunion

I RECEIVED A SPONTANEOUS PHONE CALL FROM some of my old Northwest Airline fellow employees attempting to get together for "old time's sake." I had not seen Jeff or Glenn in over fifteen years. Being back in the airline industry, serving as a Flight Attendant with Angel Air, I procrastinated due to my time spent in the air. I must admit, a part of me said, "Go, have some fun in life."

I decided to do the random nonrevenue task after I finished a four-day trip back to Denver, Colorado. Of course, all flights were sold out to Tampa, Florida. I got bumped from the first flight and waited for the next departure. Once again, the flight was full due to summer travel.

I speculated, *This isn't worth the effort sitting in the gate area.*

I was ready to go home and call it a day. Suddenly, the gate agent called out my name. He informed me that there was a possible seat available. I followed him like a lamb down the jet bridge and waited patiently for an open seat. Sure enough, he informed me to sit in 14C. I was relieved to know I made it on.

"Please shut the main cabin door!"

This was my silent prayer for any last-minute travelers. I needed to see my old friends.

Arriving sixty miles into Tampa, I had a passenger across from me who dealt with a seizure. I flung off my seatbelt and alerted the Flight Attendants seated in the rear of the aircraft on their jump seats.

"We have a passenger onboard having a medical problem," I exclaimed.

Even though I was on vacation, I assisted them to the best of my ability. The passenger was traveling alone with little information regarding his necessities. We simply pulled together as Flight Attendants to help his medical needs. The paramedics were alerted in Tampa. They did a superb job in getting this man off the aircraft. I simply put to the test my in-flight training. It did pay off. The flight crew gave me many hugs and thanked me for all my efforts.

I suppose I'm still on a vacation, even though I entailed an emergency onboard. Crews stick together no matter what!

After retrieving my baggage, Jeff pulled up at the passenger loading spot once I arrived into Tampa. I tossed my bags into his car, and off we went. We heard Glenn got bumped three times in Houston, yet we never gave up the task of being together. Sure enough, he made a later flight. Jumping from different time zones, we were all in a tizzy, wondering how we pulled this off. Glenn arrived at 10:30 p.m. I was in bed, recuperating from a six-day trip, but the sound of his voice gave me the ability to crank my body out of bed and give him a squeeze. It was time to sleep and revive our tiresome efforts. We capitalized on our old airline memories with NWA, laughed like crazy fools, and prepared for the next day. I looked like a basset hound with bags under my eyes from lack of rest, but it was worth it. The threesome was back together again, laughing about days gone by.

The next morning, we headed to the beach at Saint Pete's. Jumping over waves, capturing the sun, and slurping on a few sodas was a great delight. We had tickets to the Yankees–Devil Rays baseball game afterward. Heavens, my aging years is catching up with me, but a second wind kicked into gear for the sake of cherished friends. Coming home after a baseball victory, we spent time at the pool. I couldn't resist teaching Jeff's son a few synchronized swimming techniques to assist in his hockey future. My eyes were filled with chlorine, salt from the beach up my nostrils, and high humidity was a challenge for a gal used to the mile-high city in Denver. Needless to say, we were a bunch of kids at a slumber party.

Getting up the next day, I was in preparation for the long journey home. I got dropped off at the Tampa airport, saying our farewells in the afternoon. Little did I know, I would be picked up again due to oversold flights and no way back home. Glenn was contacting me on my cell phone to give me directions on where they were located. I ended up in a taxi parking lot, not having a clue as to my surroundings in this airport. Once again we were laughing at the crazy events that took place. Glenn made it back to Houston although I had to entail another day of sitting at the airport as a nonrevenue passenger, hoping to get onboard early the next morning. What a chore when it comes to being reunited with old buds. Sometimes you have to endure the course of action.

You never know how short life can be; therefore, a good dose of humor with old friends can lift you on a road of restoration. On route traveling home, I noticed a beautiful rainbow glowing from the Gulf to the clouds from Florida. This was an inspirational moment to reflect upon. We have many privileges working in the airline industry with free travel. It takes much patience to get through the heebie-jeebies of nonrev travel. I am thankful I had the opportunity to see my special friends. I know we'll attempt many more adventures in the near future—with Jeff working for Southwest, Glenn with Delta, and myself with Angel Air. It was a gifted moment for all of us heading to the East Coast.

I couldn't resist a state of elation in my heart, reliving these cherished times. To reconnect was a blessing. God is so gracious in His loving moment for a time-out to reduce the stress, anxiety, and hardships we can entail. I'm sure our adventures will continue, knowing we're all back in sync with one another once again.

Why I Oughta?

TRAVELING WITH MY FAVORITE FIRST OFFICER ADAM and Captain Jack, we began our journey at gate 95. It looked like Christmas, and it was only early November. Passengers were cramped together, babies screaming, dogs barking in their kennels, strollers and bags strewn everywhere. Time for a cup of java and an escape out the door. We heard our plane was at the deicing pad; therefore, we hopped in a van driven by one of our maintenance employees to pick it up. While driving on the tarmac, Jack noticed our aircraft passing us by with someone else in the driver's seat.

He inquired, "Who are those guys, and where are they going with our aircraft?"

The driver had no idea and radioed Operations to find out what was happening with our aircraft.

"All I can tell you is if this aircraft starts turning toward the runway, I might pooh-pooh a purple Twinkie," answered our driver.

Fortunately, we discovered this aircraft was returning to concourse B after passing a security clearance in concourse A. Returning from Saskatoon, Canada, is part of the US customs procedure. Two pilots on ready reserve were bringing it to the gate for us. Now we're pulling an Indy 500, racing back in the van to our gate to deliver us crew members. I hope this was no indication of how our trip series was starting off. Gate Agent Jerry left me a note on a napkin before we departed. It read, "Christmas soon." I gave him a nod of acknowledgment, smiled, and closed the door.

Our trip to Memphis, Tennessee, was smooth. We made a turn back to Denver, Colorado, then off to Winnipeg, Canada. It was so frigid; our eyelashes and nostrils froze in a matter of minutes due to exposure. We've learned how to rough it with our Canadian friends, but these temperatures were brutal. You need a polar bear to keep you warm. Adam gazed at me buried under my winter scarf and hat as we climbed into the hotel van.

My clattering teeth murmured, "Why I oughta."

Puzzled, my fellow pilots wanted to know what I meant. I explained it was an old term Grandpa Floyd taught me back in Nebraska. It symbolized that when you have no control of your situation, people are misbehaving or you experience a scornful moment, you simply resolve an opportunity to vent your emotions by uttering, "Why I oughta." With your hand clenched in a fist whirling in a circular motion, you resemble Popeye. We cackled on this new format of handling our situation when things don't go the way we planned. It already became a huge hit with the three of us.

The next day we flew from Winnipeg to Chicago, Illinois, swapped aircraft, and sat for two hours. Heading to Scranton, Pennsylvania, the weather was a warm welcome with an Indian summer in the east. We were plopped on our stools at Muggs for a bite to eat before we headed to bed. It was wonderful to toss the winter wardrobe aside after what we dealt with in Canada. Unfortunately, it's only temporary, as we got up early the next day to return to Chicago, Fort Wayne, Indiana; Chicago, then another dose of Winnipeg.

We experienced a maintenance issue in Chicago, needing a new tire—which gave us a small delay before we headed back to the frozen arctic plain. Good thing Adam had a sharp eagle eye locating safety issues with our aircraft. This also happened to be Election Day in the USA. After my predeparture announcement, I had to insert a little political humor.

"My name is Leenda, and I approve this message."

This got our passengers in hysterics. Nice to have our Canadian allies share a token of humor with the Americans. Upon our descent, a passenger asked me if her five-year-old daughter could use the restroom.

I reminded her, "We'll be on the ground in twenty-three minutes. Can she hang on?"

The mother agreed, although I noticed the little tyke's tears of misery. I needed to improvise as our lavatory door was jammed. I contacted Captain Jack to inform him of my problem in the cabin.

"Do we have to divert due to a youngster who needs the toilet?"

I replied, "No, sir, only trust me with my camping background."

He agreed. I took the little tot, handed the mom a blanket to cover the front galley, and created a makeshift lavatory in the galley with thank-you bags. Helping the little one relieve herself, I managed to get everything cleaned up, disinfected, and secured before we landed into Winnipeg. You would've thought I won the presidential election with many passengers applauding my effort in behalf of this child. I even had a comment from another passenger wondering if he could be next.

"Only if you brought your own coffee can, sir . . . Now, fasten your seat belt," I responded.

More laughter erupting from the cabin made Adam and Jack wonder what the heck was going on. Was this Leenda's stand-up comedian show onboard? Probably! Getting to our hotel room, Adam and I headed to get a burger at *Bleacher's*. Nice way to end a "Why I Oughta" day. All eyes were plugged into CNN with the election results. However, we were exhausted. We hit the hay, coming from east time zone changes. What will be is what will be. We knew by the time we arose, at 4:00 a.m., we would find out who our next president would be.

Returning to the USA, we were notified who won the election—although we had to concentrate on another quick turn from Denver to Colorado Springs before we could call it quits on this trip. It was a windy trip as another storm was brewing over the mountains. This trip was ending like it started, with juggling numerous responsibilities and confusion. There was no available gate to park; therefore, we remained in the time-out box until a gate became open. Here went the kids onboard, unlocking their seat belts to get out and roam about the cabin to use the toilet. It's suddenly Sesame Street with recess time when we were stuck on the tarmac.

For Flight Attendants, this is a difficult problem to conquer in keeping passengers in their seats. It's a federal regulation for passengers to remain seated with their seat belts secured until we arrive at the gate. Do you think anyone is paying attention? Heck, no, despite our several safety announcements. They think we're Oscar the Grouch sitting in our jump seats, but if we fail to deliver this message, this can go against us in case of a possible injury.

We were in another compromising "Why I Oughta" phase. Now we could correspond with another secret code when we see each other in the airport—simply a fun way to avoid a cantankerous mode and deliver a funny new message. It's the way to retain a tranquil spirit and stay composed during the "Why I Oughta" adversities in life.

The Nonrev Experience

WORKING AS A FLIGHT ATTENDANT, YOU GET used to the nonrevenue experience of attempting to get home or on a simple vacation due to flight loads. You have to keep your eye on the computer, for things can change in a drastic means of attempting to get onboard an aircraft. You can end up waiting for hours in the gate area, hoping for a simple seat. Plan A, B, and C are essential.

One thing I've learned is not to bother the gate agent, as I used to walk in their footsteps. I know what they are contending with. The pressure with getting a flight closed out on time with last-minute confusion is a difficult process. When you've worked the ramp, gate, ticket counter, and operations, you have a clear picture of what your fellow employees are dealing with. The last thing a gate agent wants to listen to is a nonrevenue passenger turning "psycho" when all chaos turns loose in an airport because of a full boat of passengers. Understanding this process and the patience along with it is an asset—although I must admit, nothing shocks me in this industry with last-minute changes. You can view a flight with twenty open seats the night before, dash to the airport the next day, then come to find out the flight is oversold. Groan, groan, and more groans with my vigilant exertion of energy. I'm pretty immune to any in-flight experience, but I know when to toss in the white towel when it comes to sitting in an airport all day. I'm no rookie when it comes to the airline business. It's simply a game show at the gate called *Survivor*.

To have travel privileges is indeed a blessing, although to keep a watchful eye during heavy seasonal travel peak time is a must for airline employees. I've met many disappointed employees who have waited for hours in an airport to catch a flight to their destination with time off, a vacation, or just a mere escape from life in the airline industry for a few days of peace and relaxation. We're all on the same page with trying to get out of town. Sometimes it works, and other times it doesn't. Call it a day when things don't transpire for a flight. I'm not Lady Luck when it comes to the nonrevenue practice. I've been stranded several times in airports, waiting for an available seat to get out of town.

To remain in an amicable state of mind is the key. It's not worth the turmoil to exist in perplexity while waiting for your name to be called while in the gate area. Serving as a Flight Attendant, I have the opportunity to visit many cities on my trip series. My desire to get on another plane on my days off is not my top priority. In fact, I prefer to stay home, shoot a round of golf with friends, catch a movie, go for a hike in the mountains, camp out, or write. A teeth-clenching moment in the gate area on hold can leave me in a helpless state of mind. There's much to see in my own hometown in Denver, Colorado. I look forward to being with family and dear friends while my tootsies are on the ground. Most important is that the absolute peace, serenity, and beauty of the land returns my mind to a collective state—which is very needed in my line of work. A sold-out flight or a soiled flight due to problems on the ground or in the air could be a message that I don't need to subject myself to the added stress. Fine with me. I'm getting wiser in my aging airline days. I can still entertain myself jogging around a lake with the Bee Gee's music pounding the tune "Staying Alive" into my eardrum while shaking my bootie. Now that's what I consider fun on my days off!

Entertainment Onboard

I MET CAPTAIN DARRIN ON A TRIP and was amazed at his magical tricks. It seems our flight crews are full of hidden talents, but this was one funny Captain willing to boggle your mind with in-flight Houdini movements. Darrin had a gift for me before beginning to work a flight with him: observing his levitating capacities. He arose a few inches from the ground in the front galley. Our First Officer, Jarret, performed the same tactic. I watched in deep concentration, wondering if there was an answer to this nonsense or I needed a vision test. I had him replay the act as I watched intently to figure this one out, while my fellow Flight Attendant, Mo, giggled in silence. I finally caught the mind-boggler as it all dealt within the heels.

Leaving Denver, Colorado, we were on our way into Canada. Most of our passengers traveling international did not speak any English. We had a difficult time communicating with our service. Coming to row 7, I had a lady ask me for some A-Rang-A-Tang. I wondered what she was asking me for. Isn't that an animal in a zoo? Must be time for our in-flight game show.

Picking up each item in our beverage cart, I asked her, "Would you like a Coke, Diet Coke, Sprite, pretzels, apple juice, or tomato juice?"

She shook her head in frustration.

"How about orange juice?" *Bingo!*

I hit the jackpot as she nodded her head. Whew. I've heard of *mater juice* (tomato juice), *tunic water* (tonic water), *crap apple* (Cranapple juice), or a cup of "ass" (new version of *ice*) onboard when you venture into the South, but this was a first. Just make sure you close their "winder" shade at night, bring them a pillow, and hand them a "binkie" for added comfort. Then ask them if they want a remote. It'll make their day complete.

On another trip, we had a First Officer who used to play in a band. Paul could play invisible instruments like a rock star. During our overnight in Huntsville, Alabama, he demonstrated his talent with Captain Tyler, Flight Attendant Barb, and myself. In fact, he knew the words to songs better than the DJ. We had our very own Angel Air idol onboard. What a class act!

Then there's Captain Aaron, who planted his cell phone under each one of us to kick out magical gas noises on his cell phone to First Officer Joe, Flight Attendant Kristen, and me on another overnight in Huntsville, Alabama, while driving in the hotel van. Even the van driver was in hysterics. Another trick up his sleeve was to place his cell phone over the PA system while I was in using the lavatory the next morning before we boarded our passengers. I exited the lavatory laughing so hard I had tears rolling down my face.

While traveling into Chicago, Illinois, on Easter Sunday, it was raining cats and dogs. I had a new Flight Attendant named Lisa assisting me. We parked at concourse C and naturally were leaving out of concourse F for our next flight. Scurrying from one section to another, I "biffed it" in the middle of the concourse due to a stray puddle on the floor—with my bags going every direction, along with my lunch pail splitting open with my grapes rolling across the floor. Lisa looked at me in shock.

She promptly questioned, "Oh my. Are you OK?"

Looking up, I witnessed a herd of passengers heading in my direction, ready to stomp on me if I didn't get out of the way. I rolled like a horizontal soldier in boot camp toward the gate area before I ended up like mashed potatoes.

Staring at Lisa while flat on my back, I said, "Welcome to Chicago and the airline business."

She helped me up and began to chuckle in a low tone. When we found out we had a two-hour delay for our next flight, we sat in an open gate area. Captain Bill and First Officer Mike had a contest of stripping gate tags off one another's bags and flinging them at one another during our sit. It turned into a mini archery class. With my bruised knees on ice, Lisa and I shook our heads. Boys will be boys!

How many airlines can admit their crew members are full of sideshows like I've witnessed with our Angel Airlines? Not many in my tales of travel. The things we do to entertain one another onboard or in airports are a nonstop hilarious participation. We continue to charm one another with our many outside talents. We are quite a silly family, waiting to test one another. Be grateful for the time well spent. My flight crews never cease to shock me with their comical relief during our duty time. We should be a sitcom with all we endure. Maybe that will come in the near future.

I Fought the Log and the Log Won

CAPTAIN DAVE, FIRST OFFICER ANDY, AND I were at the gate ready for our trip assignment. We were venturing to Winnipeg, Canada, after a quick turn to Idaho Falls, Idaho. I feel like I should apply for another passport due to my frequent trips to this city in Canada. I'm getting used to the frigid temperatures up north. I celebrated when we went from -56 below to -10 below. This was getting mild up here.

After we did a turn to Idaho Falls, we were finally on route to Canada. A passenger hit my green Flight Attendant button to let me know there was a problem in our lavatory. I went to check it out. There was a whirring sound when I attempted to flush out the system, including the lack of blue juice in the toilet. I grabbed two liters of water to add fluid to the dry area. Using the bottles to assist the dry pot is usually a reliable method. However, this time it wasn't. In my dire effort, I uncovered a huge "brown tree log" lodged in the cavity of the pot blocking the opening. I was sickened that this massive blockage did not go down the tube. I debated, *Did this passenger drink Metamucil today?* For it was apparent that the fiber lying in this pit was worse than a decaying redwood tree. *I've got to get rid of this ugly scene.*

I tried using another three liters to flush out the monster log. Since my bottled water did not budge the implant, I used the end of an empty water bottle as a sword to combat this beast. I felt like a gallant soldier on a battlefield. We are losing our manners with community usage of lavatories onboard. Better yet, it became a mystery of who conducted the bad deed and covered it up with rolls of toilet paper to disguise in the process. I had passengers cheering me on with my attempt to flush this tree trunk down the drain. I contacted Captain David to advise him my mission was complete. I notified him that this was not a part of my job description, yet the plumber took care of business in the cabin. The shrill flowing out of the flight deck was an amiable reply to admit, "Job well done, little lady." I'm sure I made their day complete.

Here comes round 2. I had a family traveling to Madison, Wisconsin. Poor baby boy made a mess in his diaper, filling the cabin with a disastrous odor. Dad finally got up to change his pants then decided to deposit the load in the lavatory trash can. Now, this scent had time to muster, spread, and filter through our air system. I had a frequent flyer who needed the lavatory. His eyes watered up when he opened the door. He decided to pass on this option. I then had a passenger seated in row 13B asking me to get him another Jack Daniels to oppose the smell he was exposed to. I entered the lavatory to remove this soiled diaper stinking up the cabin. I sealed it with some thank-you bags, tied it in a tight knot, and disposed of it in my front galley trash bin. Within minutes, I received a call from the flight deck.

Captain Dave asked, "Hey, Leenda, are you OK? Did you eat a bad bean burrito while on the ground?"

I responded, "Sure, guys, I'm fine but felt a need to share this aroma with you in the flight deck as we're all plugging our noses due to stench within the cabin."

Once again, more laughter in the flight deck from my fellow friends.

Round 3 was when we finished up our trip series. Running down concourse B like a bull moose, I thought I better use the restroom before hopping on the bus. Entering into an empty restroom, I opened up an empty stall. What do you think I saw on the top of the stool? You guessed it . . . another log exposed on the lid. I wanted to scream as this was a trip plagued by logs and smells of the underground. I threw in the white flag with the bowel syndrome from this trip. Now I was running for my life to escape the "Baby Ruth" fiend following me from one place to another.

Good thing I'm a mom who raised four children to know how to respond to these situations. It's an added gain serving as a crew member, for we are keen in our duties. Not to mention a natural cause, for we are immune to smelly diapers and stinky areas after taking care of our own babies. Our parental role in life, cleaning up many unforeseen messes, has converted us into "tidy bowl titans" onboard.

A Full Moon

I've ALWAYS BEEN IN TOUCH WITH A full moon's effect on traveling while working in the airline industry. I never thought this large round piece in the galaxy had such an impact on the functionality of air space and overall psyche of a day. What I've learned is that everything can go haywire, including passenger emotions. Moreover, "Little Red Riding Hood" can turn into the "big bad wolf" in minutes.

Here are some full moon tales I've survived:

"CIRCLING LIKE THE MOON"

We arrived into Madison, Wisconsin, in February 2009 and entailed a new hotel. Captain Wayne, First Officer Steve, and I grabbed a taxi, for we had arrived late into town. We had a new driver, who just got removed from his construction job in North Carolina and was now driving cabs to make a living. We can understand that issue. Josh was fairly new to his taxicab performance, but he was just a guy trying to survive. We appreciated his efforts. Little did we realize, we were about to visit Madison on a special tour in the cab. We went in several wrong directions, trying to reach our hotel room. I thought we were heading to another city in Wisconsin with the miles we were tallying up on his taxi meter. He continued to apologize for his mistakes while taking us everywhere in the city except for our actual destination. Wayne and I were in the backseat of the cab, making jovial comments while enjoying the free sights in Madison. It's no big deal for us. Why? It's because we are so used to this bounty of commotion in the air. It's actually a nice notion we're not alone with our problems we share in the air. We give a huge salute to our van or taxi drivers who escort us to and from the airport. We'll continue to appreciate their earnest performance in taking us to the airport for our showtime and thank them for lugging our black baggage.

We hope our tips help out, but if we pinch pennies until our paycheck comes through, usually we spot for one another. I hope they understand we're not a wealthy clientele as the general public thinks we are, raking in the bucks as flight crew members. This is far from the truth. We grasp any free food we can get our mighty grips on for the sake of filling up our lunch pails. Our hard work ethic is tremendous. Our payroll doesn't kick in until the main cabin door is closed. Therefore, when we board passengers, deal with special needs or problems on the ground, it is part of our responsibility. If we're stranded at airports due to mechanical or weather issues, our per diem kicks in at an astonishing rate of $1.65 per hour. So if you think we're rolling in the "green," please reconsider. This is a standard policy for many crew members serving other airline companies. Now, does that shed light on a rich crew member's income? I thought this would be an interesting fact to share. We try our best to make ends meet. My fellow friends and I would not be performing this job if we never cared, respected, and loved what we do for the sake of our passengers. Not to mention to have a company you're proud to represent is a worthy cause. This is why we hang well together!

"Full Moon Panic"

On a later flight several months later, poor Wayne had to entail another full moon with me. We were traveling from Saskatoon, Canada, when we entailed enormous thunderstorms and dealt with microbursts in our circling effort coming into Denver, Colorado. We had to divert to Casper, Wyoming, to get more fuel yet could not allow our passengers to deplane as we never passed through immigration in the USA. We tried again to get into Denver, yet it was another bouncy outcome. Once we landed at the gate, the jet bridge did not have the capacity to meet our aircraft door. We had to wait until another gate opened up on concourse A, push back, and find another gate to appease our needs.

My friends from Saskatoon kept their great nature going, for I kept them laughing about the many obstacles we were dealing with. Once we cleared customs, we had to get a bite to eat on the run. I bought some Chinese food while running through security to get to my next gate. Our next assignment was in Fayetteville, Arkansas.

Running through the airport, my box blew open. I now had rice and veggies spilled on my uniform pants. I smelled like a walking wonton, but had to get to my gate. This was embarrassing! After arriving to my gate, the agent questioned if I was the Flight Attendant working this flight.

Smelling like Chinese food, I informed her, "Yes, I'm your gal!"

I might have reeked of soy sauce, but I was there to begin boarding. After I arrived on the aircraft, I noticed a woman dressed in Middle East clothing. She was on her cell phone, speaking to her brother-in-law, informing him of our situation on route to Arkansas. I had to tell her to shut off her cell. She was compliant, yet seemed very withdrawn.

After we took off from Denver, I noticed the most beautiful full moon in my jump seat. No wonder all was going goofy today. I then began my service once we leveled off at our cruising altitude.

Suddenly, I heard a loud, *"yik, yik, eeeee"* noise. Was I hallucinating with haunting voices onboard, or had I gone over the deep end from a day plagued with hassles? I discovered the outburst was the woman dressed in Middle Eastern clothing. She immediately went into a near-comatose state of mind and a paralyzed body. In fact, I thought she was dead, slumped over on her tray table.

I scurried to my PA system to inform Captain Wayne, "You're never going to believe this, but I think someone has just collapsed or died onboard."

Wayne's reply was, "Say what? You've got to be joking. What more can happen in one day? Do what you have to, and keep me posted."

I acknowledged, "Don't worry, Wayne. I'll do what I can to revive her."

Returning to her seat, I noticed her husband pulled her up by the multiple head scarves she was wearing and began slapping her face. He grabbed a bottle of water off my beverage cart and tossed it on her body. Her response was limp.

"Uh-oh! Time to teach hubby a few lessons in civility", I thought.

My first mission was to remove her husband to a backseat so I might monitor her vital statistics. I asked him if she had a previous medical condition or on specific meds I need to know about. He enlightened me with new information.

"She's completely devastated, having just left her home country in Iran and had to tell her son and daughter farewell," he explained.

Now I understood. She was an emotionally traumatized mother. I sat beside her to rub her cheek, hold her hand, bring her some ice, strip the many garments off her overheated body, and provide some tender loving care. Asking what her name was, I proceeded to coach her.

"Hi, my name is Leenda, and I'm a mom. I'm sure you're dealing with some heartache, hardship of leaving your country and especially your children left behind. I will pray for you."

Instantly, I spotted a new revival without utilizing medical equipment. I had the capacity of simply holding another mother's hand, wiping away tears flowing from her eyes, and being near her for comfort. It was a phenomenal event due to common sense of natural and responsive human comfort, without the need of an emergency landing. I had a few passengers asking me if there was anything they could do to assist me onboard, for they knew I couldn't leave her side.

"Sure, my friends. The man in seat 8C needs a Coke, 9B needs a coffee, and 11A wants an orange juice."

What a stimulation to see these passengers help me out in a time of need to prevent an emergency landing. I do believe if you take time to listen to another person's needs, it's incredible what we can accomplish with the Good Lord's help. I did get her to come around 180 degrees with my soothing voice, hugs, and a kiss on her cheek. We landed in Arkansas without any medical emergency needs on the ground. I had several passengers give me an embrace of thanksgiving for taking care of this woman.

I knew my face was blushing and replied, "It's just my duty. We work together as a team, and I don't expect any credit. It's a joint effort. We are a united bunch when it comes to our assigned flight trip series."

Although, I must admit the full moon continues to be a trying time in the air. I'm sure Captain Wayne would love to fly with me again except during a full moon. I'm sure that will be on his bid avoid list!

"Busting into the Pearly Gates"

Here we go again with another full moon story. Gadzooks! I seem to dread the moment. It seems that we go through more garbage than any passenger can imagine during a full moon. I headed off on a trip with my buddies Captain Nick and First Officer Kara into Canada. Coming back to Denver, Colorado, we entailed another round of "microbursts" due to impending storms. This can be one of the worst turbulence adventures in the air. The more appropriate term should be labeled *busting into the pearly gates*, because the aircraft movement feels like a gigantic suction cup.

Nick called me back on the PA system and requested, "Get in your seat, Leenda, and hang on for dear life."

I bounced up and down like a fish out of water on my jump seat while watching my Saskatoon passengers resemble a bad roller coaster ride. Their bodies were getting flung to and fro in the main cabin with their seat belts on. I stayed in a silent mode of prayer for all of us yet still had to keep smiling like the Cheshire Cat in *Alice in Wonderland* to convince my passengers that all was under control. We landed into Denver in one piece safe and sound—although I must say that my nerves were shot from this nasty storm. It was a rigorous labor for all of us, yet we conquered. Sometimes these occasions can feel like an eternity while stuck in the sky.

My Canadian friends wittingly suggested, "I suppose we don't need to visit an amusement park right now . . . eh?"

I mustered a smile and bade them a lovely day. After clearing customs in Denver, we have to reposition the aircraft from concourse A back to B, and other times, our reserve pilots handle this responsibility. We dealt with a bit of confusion in our communication efforts on the ground. This is usually par during a full moon. We resembled a herd of lost sheep trying to locate one another due to our security separation. We had to sprint to get from concourse A to B for we had another flight to operate into California. Let's add a last-minute gate change to make us run further than we expected.

The only reassuring question when I arrived onboard panting and puffing was Captain Nick claiming, "Where have you been, Leenda?"

Observing his cool, calm, and collected tone of voice, I didn't know whether to kiss him or choke him.

I commented, "Well, sir, I was lost and now am found. Hallelujah!"

He gave me a wink and a thumbs up. This is what we're all about. Maybe we get rocked in the air and are ragged on the ground, yet it's our unique quality to expect the unexpected and carry on with our duty.

"Pooch on the Loose"

Another classic was with Captain Jesse. We were in San Francisco, California, ready to take off, yet a dog was running loose on the runway to stall our mission. We witnessed many red sirens on the taxiway, along with airport security, firefighters, and airport police attempting to capture the pooch. They had quite a workout, while many domestic and international aircraft were stalled, waiting for the animal to be restrained. Once again, another full moon creating havoc.

My fellow crew members never cease to amaze me in my in-flight trips. They are my best friends with a positive source of energy. If we can survive a full moon creating calamity, it proves what true "warriors" we are!

Crews Just Want to Have Fun

DESPITE OUR HURRY-SCURRY LIFESTYLE WHEN WE'RE ON a trip series, we appreciate the time to explore. Like Nancy Drew and the Hardy Boys, we are an adventurous bunch. Even though we can function on a minimal amount of rest, we manage to keep one another going to visit the sights, especially if it's a new city. Here are a few highlights:

I was with Captain Jeff and First Officer Chris in November. We stayed in Fayetteville, Arkansas, the first night. Our hotel at the time was out in the "boonies." The folks here were hospitable, although we were almost fifteen minutes from civilization—nothing but weeds surrounding us. I had a great rest, but it was an early wake-up call. That's the way it goes. The next night we were in Colorado Springs, Colorado. Yahoo for being submerged back into society! Day 2 brought us into San Jose, California, where we stepped up the pace with socializing. Talk about a transformation from the wilderness to the "wild side." This was interesting. It just happens on your flight schedule. Better get used to the drastic changes you're in for as a crew member. It makes you bendable in this business!

Then there's our bowling skills. Staying in Rockford, Illinois, Captain Matt and I thought we'd give a shot at spinning the ball down the alley. A raging snowstorm hit this area, although the van driver took us in the afternoon and planned on picking us up at 6:00 p.m. Matt and I played a game of pool. He kicked my Irish fanny in a game of pool, yet I whipped him in bowling. While waiting for the van, we could barely see one another outside the door. The howling winds and whiteout made us wonder if we were going to have a ride back to our hotel. Suddenly, a van appeared slipping and sliding through the parking lot with dim lighting.

"Glory be, she made it! She must be a female Rudolph the Reindeer," I muttered. We were relieved as it would have been a long stroll back to the hotel looking like two frozen ice cubes.

I had another adventure in Steamboat, Colorado, with Captain John, First Officer Jason, and Flight Attendant Tori. This time it was summer in the mountains. We planned on taking a rafting trip down the Yampa River, although we got delayed coming into Steamboat Springs. We decided to go bowling. We had the whole center to ourselves in Craig, where we dined on appetizers and refreshments and bowled to our hearts' content. Of course, the boys were on a competitive mission with who could knock more pins down similar to who had the best landings while descending. My jaw needed a time-out when I came home because it ached from laughing so hard due to our in-house humor, jabs, and funny episodes.

Here's another good one. Captain Neil, First Officer Mark, and my copartner, Liz, and I took off for the West Coast. We had some time in Medford, Oregon, so the van driver took us to Shenanigan's downtown. We had a bite to eat and played a few rounds of pool. It was Neil and I against Mark and Liz. I had my pool cue chalked up and ready to roll. Holy Toledo, we were worse than a bunch of college kids having some fun playing pool. Neil and I won the match. His English-born accent was another sweet reminder of the memories we had in Medford. The next morning, he contacted us before we departed Medford to inquire there was a number 2 in the lavatory.

"Do what?"

I went to inspect like the *Pink Panther*. He took a grouping of toilet paper to plant a number two on the toilet lid. Oh my. We are a crazy group!

Coming into Nashville, Tennessee, with Captain Lance, First Officer Lauren, and Flight Attendant Lois Marie during Christmas time was gratifying. The three of us ventured and toured the Grand Ole Opry decorated in a festive manner for the holiday season. We sang some Christmas tunes and enjoyed watching the "little tykes" on Santa's lap. We were amazed at the activities and the numerous Christmas decor within this building. Makes you rejoice in this beautiful season of faith, hope, and love!

My First Officer, Lauren, and I headed to Mount Rushmore while in Rapid City, South Dakota, during the month of January. Our hotel manager, Joni, was gracious to lend us her vehicle to visit the site. Lauren and I had a riot traveling through the Black Hills despite the wintertime. We were the only visitors at the site. I suppose this was an inactive time at Mount Rushmore, although we had a great time together being alone. Makes you appreciate our recorded past. Afterward, we headed down the highway. We noticed a wine-tasting event at Prairie Berry. Well, why not check this scene out? We were well informed about the berries and producing wine. What an amazing concept! We made it back into Rapid City where the manager, Joni, met us to find out what we uncovered in South Dakota. It was terrific! There's some generous folks in this area.

Working holidays are never a pleasant treat, for we crave to be at home, celebrating with our family and loved ones—although being together with crew members allows us to participate in a different fashion.

It was Valentine's Day. Captain Brain, First Officer Tim, and I were off to Saskatoon, Canada. When we arrived at the hotel, Tim was given a special key to his room attached with a love note from his fiancée, Jasmine. Brian and I wondered if Jaz came up to surprise him. When he opened the door, we resembled three little kids curious to see if she was really present. Instead, we found love notes attached to the walls in many languages saying "I Love You," a luscious cake made into a heart, and decor of Valentine's all over his room.

My Timmybits, choked up with emotion, replied, "No one has ever done this for me before."

Brian and I looked under the bed, in the shower, and closet to see if she was hiding. She wasn't there, but her spirit of love over the miles was certainly a gift. This is how we cheer one another on with an "awe" moment!

So they say a ghost lives in Wichita, Kansas, at our hotel. Well, I can assure you after my journey with Captain Joel and First Officer Matt departing the city the next day, we were plagued with mechanical problems. Sharing ghost stories in operations, we came to the conclusion that maybe this ghost didn't want us to leave after all. It was probably another fluke incident, but we tagged the disruption and delay on our graveyard "ghouls." I think our passengers enjoyed our comical quality despite our burden.

Captain Fed was another trip, along with First Officer Kelly. How we traveled through the winter storms to get to our destination. When we made it to Milwaukee, Wisconsin, we needed a time-out for one another to unwind from this trip due to many frustrating times with weather delays. No one has any idea what we crew members deal with. If you believe we have an easy lifestyle, allow a moment to reevaluate. I attempted to go work out, although some of the equipment was not in the best shape. Trying to work out on a treadmill that got stuck in high gear, I resembled *Forrest Gump* running for my life! This machine was possessed. I finally leaped off of this machine to save my soul. When we met for dinner, I informed the fellows of what happened.

They laughed and said, "Count your lucky stars, as the bicycle pedals blew off when they tried to get some cycling in."

Once again a moment of trying to stay fit on the job. I bet Jack La Lane would've condemned this workout place—yet another opportunity to grasp onto when it comes to making the best of life on the road! I think I'll trust my conditioning drills when I get home, then I know I'm working out on some safe equipment. Just another learning observation.

While in Washington with Captain Edgar and First Officer Pete, we spotted a karaoke sign. We decided to give it a shot at our hotel, for Edgar loves to sing. Little did we know, upon entering, we were outnumbered by a rambunctious crowd. They obviously had been partying for quite some time, yet we were clean. It was a table-dancing event, with chairs falling over and much rough language getting flung across the room. Needless to say, we excused ourselves in a quick means. It would be difficult to explain to crew support the next day how we witnessed a tough crowd at our hotel. Time for the hotel key and a safe means behind closed doors. I watched some television instead to pacify a lost singing moment for some nighttime entertainment.

Heading in and out of Aspen, Colorado, with Captain Colby, First Officer Tim, and Flight Attendant Ashley was a struggle. These men are the Aspen pros and could land the flight blindfolded due to their expertise at this airport, for it can be demanding during the winter months. The next night, we were in Phoenix, Arizona. It felt great to have some warmth and not battle snow, ice, nor wind. We took a hike along the campus and dined on some awesome Mexican food. It's a joy to strip off the boots, mittens, and coats during the winter months. We appreciated the short-lived moment. Coming into Los Angeles, California, it was another stunning time on day 3. Hard to imagine people are struggling with warming up their cars in the morning when we get an opportunity to bathe in the sunshine. Naturally, our final fourth day was a "humdinger." That's pretty typical when we want to go home.

Departing Los Angeles, I had a passenger who appeared very nervous. She was shaking upon entering the aircraft, spilled her purse in the front galley, and numerous pills rolled out under my feet. She explained she just got out of rehabilitation and needed to get home. She had a doctor's note to confirm her ability to travel, but she was a handful. I informed Colby and Tim of her uneasy nature onboard. When we were pulling out of the gate, she needed many sick bags. Both Ashley and I monitored her behavior. During our taxiing and ascending, she got out of her seat to head to the restroom while the seat belt signs were still activated. Ashley informed her she needed to take her seat, but this gal was totally out of sorts. We had to keep our pilots informed of what we were contending with on route to Oklahoma City, but they knew we had it under control. Good thing we enjoyed our time on the ground in nice climate, for we never know what we're in for flight after flight. It's all a mystery, but our bonding together gets us through the insanity times.

It was a beautiful fall day in Missoula, Montana. Together with my crew members Captain Justin, First Officer Tony, and Flight Attendant Lori, we decided to climb the "M." It's a lot steeper than it looks near the campus at Missoula, although the crew trudged forward. I made it halfway then decided I wanted to check out the city. As a former tour leader, I enjoy checking out the "hood" for a place to eat and enjoy some thirst quenchers. We hit Red's and met some of the locals. Their congeniality in Montana is admirable.

The next day we left for Eugene, Oregon—another one of my favorite places. We took a seven-mile ride on the banks of the river then dined on some appetizers at El Torrito. My dear friend Karim deadheaded on our flight, so she joined in on the merrymaking. It was a warm sunny day in Eugene, vibrant in color with shades of green. OK, time for bed, as we have an early rise and shine.

The next day we were in Edmonton, Canada—quite a switch from the warm weather we were spoiled by. It doesn't matter when you're with a great crew. Laughter will always warm the heart and soul. Attempting to locate a place to dine, we crossed the street several times, shielding us from the windy buffets.

Finally, Justin blurted out, "Why did the crew member cross the road?"

We stared at him in disbelief but responded, "To get to the other side."

Therefore, we decided on some good ole Italian "grub." After nibbling on some tasty pizza, I probably could use another workout on the "M"—but a superior time with friends.

How can anyone who's flying with Captain Randy be miserable, for he was Mr. Absurdity Man of Angel Air! Together with First Officer Greg, the three of us were off on a trip to the east. Chicago had its normal congestion, but we made the best of it. I got to attend my first walk-around with Greg, so now I understand their required routine with checking out an aircraft before each arrival and departure. We like to call it the runaround when our poor First Officers deal with frigid temperatures.

I just finished telling Randy about my "Love Taps" story when we were ready to board. Talk about a coincidence, as here comes an extremely large passenger seated in a bulkhead seat. Poor guy needed not only an extension belt, but had a difficult time squeezing into our seat and smashing his neighbor's head into the window. He was very cordial regarding his size and apologized for flowing out of his seat, yet blocking my ability to break out my beverage cart.

I advised him, "It's fine. I'll make it work."

I started the sidewinder dance with my cart, attempting to finish my service on this short flight. I noticed this man was standing in my galley halfway through our flight. I needed some tea, but he took up most of my space in trying to get a hot cup of water. I asked him if he was OK.

He replied, "No, madam, I'm just fat."

Oh dear. I couldn't lie and say, "No, you're not," but I had a better method in making him feel comfortable, special, and needed.

"Well, sir, look at this way . . . you're a bundle of love onboard. That's all that matters in life."

He gave me a sly grin and thanked me for my kindness. Now, that's not so hard, is it? We as humans can poke fun at life, but we need to share a common courtesy and sensitivity when it comes to being with one another in close quarters. I prefer to consider this as a time to "get to know your neighbor" with some spunk in your seat.

Once we landed into Charleston, West Virginia, the front desk told us to go check out a fun sports pub called Sam's. While dining on some fine food, Randy had both of us in hysterics with his one-liners as a veteran. We thanked our fine hostess for an enjoyable atmosphere and headed back to the hotel for a good night's snooze. The next day we ventured into Casper, Wyoming, and contended with some high winds. We hid in our rooms and watched movies. The hotel van was in the shop getting repaired on our last day; therefore, we took a cab to the airport. Randy's front seat was in a reclining mode, which hit my knees and Greg's in the backseat. In the meantime, Randy kept on yakking to this poor young man, who looked like he just got home from "Woodstock." Shucks, we don't care about anyone's outside appearance. We're grateful for a quick spin to the airport and love to share our stories with others.

Captain Bryan, First Officer Andrew, and I were taking off for Sioux Falls, South Dakota. When I arrived onboard to introduce myself, Bryan was already doing a mean "boogie" behind the steering wheel. *Uh-oh, this could be another wild and crazy four-day excursion,* I contemplated, but let's have some fun, gang!

I took Andrew on a hike in September to view the falls. It was pretty dried up since my last visit in April, although still a remarkable view. We ventured to Saint Joseph's Cathedral, where they were renovating the church. We managed to squeeze in a side door and had an opportunity to see the interior with its beautiful paintings and statues. Fantastic! How we loved gazing at the beauty of this Cathedral. It brought back memories of my time in Paris visiting Notre Dame Cathedral. Leaving the church, we hiked through the historical district. The homes are very Victorian yet well preserved. In the meantime, Bryan was waiting for me at Wiley's, a local establishment near our hotel. Go figure, it was ladies' night with free appetizers. No wonder he wanted me to show up for a freebie. Time for some rest.

The next day we traveled in and out of Chicago, Illinois. Our body clock went from Central time to Eastern three times in one day.

By the time we arrived in Wisconsin, it felt like, "What's up in Wausau?"

Landing, I got on my PA system and replied, "Ladies and gentlemen, welcome to . . ." Pause. I had no idea where I was at due to six legs in the air.

A passenger sitting in my front row stated, "You're in Wausau."

I replied, "Oh, thank you, sir. The local time here is, um . . ." Pause.

He retorted, "Leenda, you're in Central time."

By then I had the whole cabin bursting into a frenzy of laughter. They understood we had a long day. We stayed in a cozy hotel decorated with bears, fish, and even a doe-and-buck for a restroom. How clever. I watched Bryan do a little country jig down the hallway. I put in a good two-step, and we bade one another a good night. That's how we jive!

My fellow football buds are another story. Being raised in Nebraska the majority of my life, I'm still a huge Husker fan, even though I've resided in Colorado for many years. My airline friends on the ground with Angel Air don't like me very much when it comes to the "pig-skin season," but my fellow Nebraska Captains—Chad, Alan, and John—do. It's all in good fun, as we rib one another game after game at the gate before take-off.

I was with Chad in Canada when Nebraska had their opening game in September 2007. I remember the poor guy went up and down the street, desperately searching for a television to capture the game. He was so distraught and blurted, "What's the matter with you people? It's opening day for college football, and all we get to do is watch hockey up here!"

We never got the scores until the next day traveling back to the USA. My fellow Flight Attendant, Patty, could not believe the undertaking we were on to get a score on NU although her team, USC, was playing also. We were all curious with our favorite team's outcome. That's the tough part as crew members. We enjoy our sports like our Canadian comrades!

Misery is when you get stuck in a city for a long duration. This happened to Captain Joseph, First Officer Davie, and myself. We spent thirteen hours in Fort Wayne, Indiana, waiting for our updated news regarding the weather conditions in Chicago, Illinois. We were up at four in the morning, ready for our assignment, but the rest of day went bleak. Joseph, Davie, and I had a bite to eat and waited for some answers regarding our trip. It was one long day, but we managed to make it through by sharing some of our infamous in-flight stories as crew members. No, it's never an easy project, for we want to head home as bad as our passengers—although sometimes we are stranded like you. We do what we can to make the best of a miserable situation. It is a part of our training and endurance to keep us going in a forward motion. We have our good days and our frustrating ones. I must admit: this was one of the longest delays I've entailed, working with Angel Air. Once again it was a great notion to have my fellow crew members be in happy spirits despite the agony with delays in Chicago. That's a great attest in perseverance!

With an overnight in Albuquerque, New Mexico, Captain Chris, fellow Flight Attendant Olivia, and I took off on a bus to capture some fine Mexican dining the next day. It was a spectacular fall day on the campus. We strolled the sights, took funny pictures, and landed a place near a lake to absorb the sunshine. With our shoes off basking near the lake, pants rolled up, we got engrossed in some heavy topics on life. We covered relationships, our direction in life, and conversation with where we're going, what we are doing, and what is meant to be.

Chris paused for a moment and asked us, "Do you think this is a Dr. Phil moment?"

After hearing this, Olivia and I cracked up with his suggestion. That's the unique portion of being a crew member. The harmony we develop week after week from traveling together is held in high esteem. We lose precious time at home with our families and friends, yet have to create a new family being on the road. We get used to being nomads in the air.

Traveling with Captain Alex and First Officer Jeff on many destinations, we dove into the dilemma of where are we going, for I don't remember where and what time it is. This is a common denominator with crew members, as we can be in several cities in one day, changing many time zones. We have to keep one another informed as we can be "lost in space" due to our many rapid changes. First Officer Jeff and I had an opportunity to capitalize on some free appetizers while in Idaho Falls, Idaho. He was puzzled due to my ability to recall crew members' names and adventures in the air. I informed Jeff, being a writer is no different than a photographer, musician, or an artist. Some may label me as an offbeat lady, but it's a gift to share with others. I might be considered odd, but I have a great capacity of storing information absorbed with details locked into my memory bank. I may not remember where I'm coming or going on my next trip series, but when it comes to a traveling experience with fellow crew members, my recollection is unbelievable. Writers have an opportunity to unveil many truths about the quality in life.

We had a good overnight in Eugene, Oregon, with my fellow Flight Attendant Amber, First Officer Matt, and Captain Eric. I've been in Eugene many times and have ridden the bike up and down the trail, paid homage to the Duck's stadium, yet I've never seen Oregon. The three of us decided to rent a car and go visit the Oregon coast. I've never seen anything so elegant with its rich shades of green and beautiful coastline. Like three little siblings, Matt, Amber, and I played on the beach, collected seashells, watched sea lions frolic in the ocean, and admired the beauty of the landscaping. It reminded me of my travels in Ireland, with its abundance of green scenery. I was impressed. It was worth the effort, even though we are usually tired coming into a city. Sometimes we have to ignite a spark under one another as we usually want to hide out in our hotel room and make up for lost snoozing. This time it was a true motivation on our behalf as the sack sounded too tempting, although we can always rest when we get home. To live like a "doer"—as Matt calls it—is worth the energy!

Going back into Omaha, Nebraska, on my recent trip in April 2010 with Captain Tim and First Officer Kyle was another sentimental moment. I was their official tour guide, showing them the "hot spots" in downtown "Big O." My high school friends came to join us. We soaked up the April sunshine on top of a deck at the Old Market. The guys took it in stride, while the ladies reminisced down memory lane. Leaving early the next morning, I noticed my old Northwest Airlines counter was now replaced with Angel Air. I asked the general manager if he would allow me to view the back room for old times' sake.

When he opened up the back room, all I could say to him was, "If these walls could talk, you'd have quite another novel brewing, as this was the beginning of my career in the airline industry since 1983."

He gazed at me with a funny nod of acknowledgment. To see many changes at this airport was a déjà vu time for me. I've witnessed many changes and have endured many layoffs, downsizing, strikes, and mergers in this industry. Nevertheless, my airline friends have always been a true life support system. They'll continue to be a vital part of my happiness as I continue to serve as a Flight Attendant. I'll never regret my days of getting trampled as a ramp, ticket, baggage, or gate agent on the ground.

Another good tale is when Captain Kris, First Officer Laura, and I landed into Springfield, Missouri. We had an opportunity to visit Branson, although this was Veterans' Day. Most of the vets had all cars rented, so we decided to stick close to our hotel and venture to Ruby Tuesday for some fine dining. Laura's boyfriend, Bob, came to join us. The four of us studied the menu. We looked like four college kids working out a plan with the price of one free entrée and one paid meal. We dined like a bunch of fine diplomats on a cheap budget, conversing in home improvements, relationships, going boating, and making a living one day at a time. I wish I would've had a recorder for the many humorous one-liners we shared together. That's what's unique about crew members. We always assist one another through dirt-poor conditions.

Our PA communication can be a side splitter, depending on whom you're traveling with.

With Captain Vance and First Officer Ryan, upon usage for requesting special needs, I dealt with, "Hello, front desk, Papa John's, what is your order?" or "If there's a problem with this reception, please press 1."

But my favorite was hearing from my Salt Lake Captain, Chad, and Denver-based First Officer, Eric. They responded, "Hello, this is the Bat Cave. Batman and Robin are busy at the moment, but if you leave me your name, number, and time you contacted us, we'll be happy to get back to you as soon as we can."

Traveling from Denver, Colorado, to Burbank, California, I was collecting trash. A lady passenger had a man seated next to her with an empty cup between his legs sound asleep.

"Go ahead, I dare you to pick this up."

I replied, "No, I double-dog dare you to attempt this mission in my behalf."

We both cackled over this plan of action. I finally caught this man in his awakened state to hand me his cup in a proper manner, yet the gal next to him kept on laughing.

"Hey, Leenda, look me up when you come into Burbank next time around. I'm sure we'd have way too much fun together."

While in Reno, Nevada, we had an opportunity to test our luck at a few machines for Captain Aaron's birthday. First Officer Chris and I sat on stools with Aaron and played a few poker games. I'm a lousy gambler, so I decided to work the penny machines. It's more fun anyway. I chose the Frog Prince game. Funny thing is, I kept winning for kissing the video frog while gaining points. Story of my life, I suppose—never a prince, just many frogs in the lineup.

I chose to do an overnight in San Francisco, California, over New Year's Eve. My fellow crew members—Captain Ryan, First Officer Matt, and Flight Attendant Jill—were assigned this trip. I decided this would be a great way to bring in the New Year. Reaching San Francisco around 7:30 p.m., we made a plan to meet in Jill's room. Her husband, Ben, drove in from Chico, bringing snacks for us to feast on. There were a few other crews in town; therefore, all of us met on the lower level to share more airline stories. Suddenly, I heard some music in the distance. Out of curiosity, I took Matt with me to go scope it out. It was a company party, yet we decided to join in on the festivities. Matt and I got a few Latin moves on the dance floor with our new San Francisco friends.

When we returned to our crew members, they asked, "Where have you been?"

I replied, "Oh, we were just getting our shaker going to bring in the New Year."

When the clock struck twelve o'clock, all the hotel guests yelled out in merriment, "HAPPY NEW YEAR!"

Now, that's how you bring in a holiday on the right foot.

After a rough go in the air, Captain Mike, First Officer Lem, and I headed downstairs in the hotel for some karaoke in Grand Junction, Colorado. We needed some earplugs for a few singers, yet there were some talented individuals.

Naturally, my crewmen wanted to jump on the stage. I proposed that I only sing well in the shower, but they didn't care. Therefore, they chose the song "You Don't Bring Me Flowers Anymore." Mike started us off with a Louie Armstrong tone of voice, while Lem and I chimed in the background. I must admit: it would've made the original artists cringe at our musical debut, but we unleased our talent.

Returning to Denver the next day, Lem contacted me to check on the status of the cabin's security.

I expressed, "Cabin is secure, but you don't bring me flowers anymore."

Off we flew with another good chuckle to start our day flowing on a positive note.

Where's the Love?

I ENTAILED A FEW COUPLES RETURNING FROM Hawaii into Los Angeles. They were traveling into San Jose. One was a newly married couple. They couldn't keep their hands off on another.

They asked me for a blanket, and I replied, "Sure enough, just behave yourself onboard." They both giggled.

Next is a troop of twelve in their 'sixties, who finished a vacation with their husbands and fellow friends. The ladies were in the back of my aircraft and the men in the front.

I attempted to seat them together, but in the process, the ladies retorted, "Don't you dare. We're sick of their ugly faces and need a time-out."

Oh boy. When I approached the men to explain my situation in seating them next to their spouses, they voiced, "You keep those ladies as far back on the bus as possible."

What a contrast from the refreshing "newlyweds" onboard and the ones who've been married for many years. Talk about a switch. I think the guys would've skinned me alive if I placed them next to their loving spouses during our flight. *Yikes* . . . Just another funny scene to witness.

Now I have to deal with the many electronic devices. Traveling from San Francisco into Burbank, which is a short flight, I entailed a forty-year-old passenger not willing to turn off his cell phone. I informed him five times to turn off his device as we were departing San Francisco. Doing my final sweep of the cabin, this passenger was not in his seat but underneath the seat in front of him, trying to hide like a three-year-old kid. Like I'm not going to catch him on my flight in small quarters? I think not. Here comes the mom mode inside of me.

With my hand on my hip, I explained, "Give your cell phone to me, for you've been a naughty boy on my flight. You'll get your device back when we arrive into Burbank."

He looked at me with eyes of astonishment, but he knew I meant business. I had many passengers clapping in my attempt, for they followed the rules, but this passenger took it over the limitations.

I had one passenger exclaim, "Where's the love, Leenda?"

I suggested, "I'm not sure, my friend, but I will spread the love until you cross my boundaries. Then I become a woman on a course of operation. Just the way I handle business in the air!"

My favorite love story is when I came into Great Falls, Montana, before Christmas a few years ago. I had a passenger by the name of Gloria coming to see her long-lost friend, Wally. Both of them had endured past losses of their spouses and were going to see one another after many years of separation. Gloria showed me a few treasured items of jewelry Wally had bestowed upon her over the years. She bought a one-way ticket from Atlanta to see her loving mate. I enlightened her for being a brave woman. How she giggled.

Landing in Great Falls, I did my usual required announcements yet couldn't resist to inform my passengers of a great Christmas love story. How the crowd roared with my story to wish Gloria the best in life. My Captain Erik contacted me to ask what the noise was about in the cabin. I notified him it was a Christmas miracle! Our crew had to go investigate. Sure enough, Wally was at the baggage claim area, decked in a fine outfit with a dozen roses and box of candy for Gloria. I couldn't resist in introducing myself as a Flight Attendant in her behalf. I simply proposed that he better take care of her, "As there are forty-nine people watching you right now, pal." How he laughed. They both departed the terminal hand in hand while all my passengers gave them a huge round of applause.

Now, that's love, my dear friends. I still post passengers on my flights to Great Falls this heart-warming gathering. It still makes them smile and me too!

You Don't Say?

MONITORING SEVERAL NEEDS ONBOARD, I GET A charge from the numerous expressions with my passengers and fellow crew members. These are a few of their remarks I've logged in my memoirs to share.

Traveling into Aspen, my First Officer, Chris, had his mom and dad on our flight. When Chris made his PA announcement, his mom—in a moment of excitement—yelled out loud, "That's my boy." Passengers looked at me in a puzzled daze, but I could relate to her proud moment with her son flying our aircraft. I would've done the same thing if it were one of my boys. It's just a mom thing we share together.

While in Cody, Wyoming, watching my Captain, Chad, run to and fro to get our aircraft ready to depart, he called out, "Why didn't I become a dentist?" Lord, have mercy. Well, why didn't I become a dental assistant myself? I guess the Good Lord wanted us to become crew members instead. It's called dealing with the "fold."

While in flight to Denver, a passenger, George, from the South asked me, "Hey, lady, I think the Captain missed his turn for the landing spot, for he just passed by the airport."
My reply was, "I think he knows where he's going, sir. Just relax for now. He has a special map in the flight deck to land this aircraft

in a safe means. It's not a road map on a highway, but similar in the air. If you spot any sand, then let me know. It means we're heading for Las Vegas instead."

One passenger yelled out, "Now, that sounds like more fun than my business meeting!"

George looked at me with a bewildered gaze and responded, "OK, lady, I'll trust in your advice and reassurance that they know what they're doing up front."

I informed him with a grin, "I taught them well, my friend."

While conducting my exit row information speech, I had a passenger inform me he lifts 190 lbs. every day when he escorts his woman to a nearby restroom. His wife smacked him upside the head when he shared this information. I had to contain my snickering.

She shouted, "He's all yours, honey."

I reminded her, "No, my dear, he's your problem child. I already raised my four."

While waiting for the ramp personnel to deliver their cargo report to Captain Carsten in Huntsville, he was occupied doing his figures for weight and balance. Upon delivery, he remarked, "Here you go, sir. Now you do da voodoo!"

Traveling from Wichita to Chicago, we had a group of World War II vets onboard. All dressed in bright yellow T-shirts, with matching hats, they were traveling to a special dinner to be honored for their time of service in Washington, DC. I've never dealt with more canes, wheelchairs, walkers, and hearing aids in my years as a Flight Attendant—although they all looked so cute. When conducting my beverage service, I needed a megaphone to communicate since most of them couldn't hear me.

"Speak up, honey, what did you say?"

I leaned over and expressed, "How about cranking up your batteries, gentlemen. Then we can correspond in a proper manner without me yelling." They got a charge out of that remark.

On route to Aspen, a young twelve-year-old came onboard and asked me if we were planning on televising the soccer cup finals.

When the flight deck heard this one, they listened intently to my reply, "Sure, kiddo, just push the button on your seat. An instant DVD player with HD will satisfy your needs during this twenty-minute flight." Another grin.

I don't know how many times I've heard this one, but while performing my head count with my PIN pad, I get asked, "I'll take bacon and eggs over easy, steak medium rare, and easy on the hash browns."

My response is a quick-witted one. "How about pretzels, or a cookie for an entrée instead?"

While traveling to Rapid City, I engaged in a lively conversation with my passengers regarding the Mount Rushmore monument. Captain Cliff and First Officer Mason attempted to get me close over the hills so I could witness this sight from above on the EMB. All I could see were rocks.

Passengers answered, "Well, that's because it's over on this side."

I tried to retain my balance and capture a panorama, but before I knew it, we had passed the historical sight. Hmmm. This can be the disadvantage of being a Flight Attendant. The guys and gals have a much better picture window in the flight deck than I do. They get an opportunity to witness many beautiful sunrises and sunsets with Mother Earth, while we're stuck in the back of the bus, getting our service items prepared.

This is life, but I do catch some pretty nifty views when I can. We're just another step closer to heaven in my book. Unfortunately, when passengers ask me what lake we just flew over or what mountain range that was, I'll submit a sigh of uncertainty.

I don't have a GPS handy, but possibly a geography book would be helpful. If I don't know the territory we're flying over, I can ask the pros in the flight deck. They usually let me know or make up some sarcastic area to pass on. I find it rather humorous when we're heading to the West Coast, passing over Lake Tahoe, and they inform me it's Lake Erie. It depends on who I'm flying with. If I have First Officer Alan onboard, who is a college professor in geology at CU, he will keep me posted on every sediment on this earth we're flying over. Best of all, there's no exam with Alan.

An elderly passenger from Denver to Cedar Rapids asked me for a cup of coffee. He shuddered, covered his head, and in a timid means, asked me if he could also have an orange juice.

I questioned, "Do I look like Medusa, sir, with snakes coming out of my head when requesting a second item? Please don't tell me you've been treated like this on a flight. If so, I am very sorry this has taken place, for we don't treat you this way on Angel Air."

He gave me a sweet grin, thanked me for my services provided, and gave a gigantic squeeze when he deplaned. It's the little gestures in life which are significant!

Coming into Palm Springs in December with Captain Eric and First Officer Matt was a highlight with warmer temperatures to enjoy. Getting off our flight on route to the terminal, a passenger was screaming much strong and vile language, being lost and heading to the wrong gate area.

Eric replied, "Just calm down," while Matt and I were astonished due to this person's temper.

Attempting to leave the airport, another passenger crossed the security line, setting off alarms while looking for her husband. She didn't speak English, yet here comes the patrol to figure out what the heck is going on with what she triggered off. Welcome to Palm Springs!

Finally, I can override the small obstacles, but to be a lamb in a lion's den is a chore onboard. Here's my version of the **Ten Commands** while flying with us. It's what my ears are used to hearing and a few minor suggestions:

1. Ye shall not whine, "It's too hot or too cold non-stop. We're trying to make you comfortable due to the many rapid changes we contend with. Be patient!"

2. Ye shall not ask, "Don't you have anything better to eat on-board?" Tossing your left-overs into my ice bucket for three points when I'm not aware, is not appropriate. Save your game for your home or office entertainment.

3. Ye shall not steal another passenger's wheelchair we ordered on the ground, nor a pillow, blanket or one of our safety cards as a souvenir.

4. Ye shall be grateful with, "Where's the space I paid for?"

5. Ye shall not tell a white lie with, "This bag fit on the last plane".

6. Ye shall not condemn our youthful spirit with, "How old are your pilots? I don't see any gray hair in the flight deck. Did they just get their driver's license?"

7. Ye shall not be biased with, "What's a woman doing behind the controls of this aircraft?"

8. Ye shall love thy neighbor instead of, "Oh this is such an "itty- bitty" aircraft then the last one I was on and the person next to me is too close for comfort!" Deal with a new cozy zone.

9. Ye shall honor a crew member's request when turning off all necessary portable electronic devices during critical flight stages. Trying to hide your "goodies" under a blanket or winter coat while sending a secret message, your Pink Panther Flight Attendant will catch you.

10. Ye shall give a shout of praise, thanksgiving and a kind word knowing we got you safely to your destination. Don't thank us, but a Divine grace from above. We are simple servants with trained wings. This is what we represent and conduct on behalf of our passengers with Angel Air!

"Swing Your Crew Member Round and Round"

WE WERE TO DEPART ON AUGUST 2010 for our four-day trip duty out of Denver. Our Captain, Steve, wasn't feeling well and had to escape several times before our departure. He was pulled off the trip, and my First Officer Eric, and I had to undergo a mechanical hassle. Our trip to Grand Junction was canceled. We headed to Burbank, not knowing who our Captain was to be; but lo and behold, we received John from Los Angeles.

We arrived into Burbank a tad late, and my left eye was throbbing. I think I caught "pink eye" from a passenger. Good thing I carry drops in my flight bag. I was up most of the night, placing eye drops in my eye and using a warm washrag for the "goop." I contacted crew support to give them a heads-up on my physical condition. They were great in responding to my needs. I felt O.K. the next day, but still concerned about my health issues. Oh, well, here I go on route to San Francisco. Now my right ear is plugged up, and I can barely hear what passengers are requesting. Lord, have mercy on my feeble body for now. I was informed our jet service into Medford was downsized to a thirty-passenger turbo-prop when we arrived into San Francisco. The First Officer sat ready while I took off with a Fresno-based crew. They had to give me a brief lesson as I've not operated this aircraft in over three years. God help me to remember what to do as I am qualified, although I don't operate this aircraft out of Denver anymore. Like riding a bike, it all came back to me, and I handled it well, thanks to my Fresno, California crew members. When I arrived back into SFO, we had another Captain taking us to Ontario, California. Traveling back the next day, we had another Captain in charge from Tucson. Phil kept us laughing in SFO. The only consistent thing was Eric and myself on this trip series.

On my trip with Captain Warren and First Officer Brandon, we traveled over tornadoes in Illinois and Wisconsin during November while heading to Pittsburgh. There was lightning all around us, but we had a safe landing regardless of the imminent storm ready to hit this area. Going back into Minneapolis, we entailed snow, wind, ice, and cold. I was trying to physically prepare myself for -2 in Bismarck North Dakota, for we just departed a city where it was in the sixties. Arriving into Bismarck, I think my body went into a temporary state of shock. *Is this some type of bad dream?* I puzzled over.

We ran to the hotel van, while slipping and sliding on the snow-packed roads, and asked our driver to crank up the heat. When it gets this drastic in temperature changes, all you want is a bed, heat, and many blankets to revive your system. We left the next day back to Minneapolis, Minnesota and found out our next flight had been canceled. We had twenty minutes to get to our next flight they were deadheading us on. We raced from concourse A to E. Of course, the wheel on my crew bag split, which made it even more difficult in my marathon attempt. To top it off, this was Thanksgiving week—with travelers packing the airport with all their bags, hustling back and forth. By the time we arrived at the gate, our flight was closed out. Now what? Another call into crew support for Captain Warren, O.K. plans had changed. We're going to spend the night in Minneapolis, take a flight into Chicago in the early morning, then catch another one to San Francisco to hook up with our originating trip series into Oregon. Is this the beginning of a "joyous holiday" season? I'm beginning to wonder.

Another tale of woe was heading into Montana, Utah, New Mexico, Georgia, and Texas over Super Bowl XXV. The first week of February was plagued with many cancelations due to an extreme weather system affecting major cities and states over the nation. Never have I witnessed so many abolished flights, but crew members as well as passengers were stranded from coast to coast. We were tossed like a volleyball with our assigned schedule. All was subject to change at this point. Houston was shut down due to ice, yet Dallas was limited due to seven inches of snow while staggering flights. What a mess, with many passengers coming into town for the "big game." Our First Officer, Javier, turned into a running back with his walk-around while inspecting the aircraft in bitter, cold temperatures. Poor guy was from Los Angeles. No wonder he darted so swiftly, creating a new airline record on the ground—which I'd prefer to label as a runaround with needed long johns. We did manage to perform our Atlanta turn back into Houston, although we missed our deadheading flight to Denver. Our weary bodies made it back to the hotel by midnight. We had to get up at 4:00 a.m. to catch a 6:00 a.m. flight. Going through security, I resembled a defensive player in the Super Bowl, trying to get to our gate. Captain Jim simply chuckled at this old goat's ability to kick my Irish heels into high motion. I'm unleashing my energy source for this is "heading home" after traveling for seven days. We're all worn out from the bitter cold.

Once again I salute my fellow crew members noted as the "Three Musketeers." We manage to pull off our trip series with much poise, joy, and professional attitude despite the congestion we deal with. I did perform the dance well by swinging my fellow airline crew buds round and round. I'd like to call it not the "hustle," but maybe the "airline two-step shuffle" is more appropriate. We perform the dance quite well in this business! We'll be happy to give lessons onboard. Please allow us to warm up our bones first.

Bags Onboard

It seems like I screen more passengers attempting to try the sly-dog method with cramming oversize bags onboard than an inspector for TSA. They may have been able to slip by the gate agent, but the grizzly bear Flight Attendant will nab you. I refer to it as my cabin border patrol mission. They don't like me patrolling the aisles, checking for bulging bags, blocking the entrance and exit area for safety purposes with FAA obligations we have to abide by. I've busted many tactics, for they test my ability and squeeze their belongings into the overhead bins and underneath the seat, which doesn't comply. Many passengers become agitated because their swelling material will not fit in our "teeny-weeny toy aircraft." I've witnessed passengers using their heads, legs, and even standing on another passenger's armrests for the jamming procedure. This can quickly turn into a *Romper Room* atmosphere, where passengers attempt to hide bags between their legs, under winter coats, or blankets—Stashing in the lavatory is another slick move. Yes, this has transpired.

Here comes the big complaint: "Well, it fit on the last flight I was on!"

What rolls around in my thoughts is, *It probably did, and I'm sure it was a 757 aircraft.*

Silence is golden at times. Yes, we're not a large carrier, but we are accommodating for your needs. "Let's all get along and be snug," is a crew member's advice. Allow me to place a gate check tag on your bag to relieve your misery. You can pick it up when you arrive at your destination, either on the jet bridge or the ramp cart. It's a simple procedure, although I must admit, people are afraid of letting go of their carry-on baggage. I can sympathize, as I used to work in baggage service. I know the misfortunes that can take place. In turn, passengers need to understand the FAA restrictions. We are measured with an effort to enforce and comply with safety hazards. In addition, we have weight and balance restrictions. Removing bags, and sometimes passengers, is not a jovial ordeal either but can be a necessity before take-off.

Most travelers are good, although we've all had a few obstinate characters who will try to sneak on unbelievable carry-on items. I've accommodated many passenger goodies within my own personal Flight Attendant compartment onboard to put their needs at ease. We've helped many brides-to-be with their bulky wedding gowns, tuxes, suits for a special occasion, and fragile items due to a family member's loss. We do what we can to provide for our special passengers; although keep in mind, we are limited to complete the boarding process. Time is essential for us as crew members. We're racing against the clock to entail an on-time performance. A connection is just as vital to our passengers as it is for the flight crew. It's all about retaining the peace onboard with bags because they are essentially every passenger's travel necessity!

Hotels . . . Seven Lessons to Abide By

RESIDING IN HOTEL ROOMS EVERY WEEK IS not what it's cracked up to be. If you're a Johnny come-lately fresh and new in the business, I reflect a world synonymous with a utopia. You don't have to make your bed in the morning, can flip several channels with your handy remote, sip on a cup of coffee, or read your favorite book. Allow me to enhance this subject with a few realistic accounts. This ultimately led me to lay out a few proactive rules relating to lodging in hotels:

Lesson 1: Flashlights are not only part of our FAA required items, but also for our bed and surroundings.

I woke up one morning in Arizona and had bites all over my back and arms. I was scratching like a pup on route to the airport for our morning show time. My First Officer, Andrew, asked, "What's wrong? You act like you've got fleas munching on your skin like it's a buffet?" When I lifted up my shirt sleeve he observed the many bites I had inherited. "Holy Moly, you've been exposed to bed bugs!" he exclaimed. Bed bugs? I hesitantly inquired, "Where do bed bugs come from?" Andrew subsequently proceeded to tell me that in certain area's we travel to, they can be a common factor amongst hotel dwellers. "Does this mean I have to start packing Raid in my crew bag?" I asked him. His reply was, "No my dear, just use your flashlight and search the headboard first, turn down your bedding for that's their hide-out when you can witness the critter's race across your bed." O.K., now I was paranoid.

Lesson 2: Always make sure you have your room key with you, check for sliding bars on your balcony and make sure your will is updated.

Have you ever been locked out of your room while leaving your hotel key inside? This happened in Salt Lake City, Utah, on a brisk February evening. I was speaking to my second son on my cell phone, yet my reception was jumbled. I decided to head out on the slim balcony to hear his voice and wish him well. When I attempted to re-enter my room the security bar slipped down, leaving me with a few inches to squeeze by. I was trapped outside in ten degree temperatures, while nursing a bad cold and frantically calling for help. Naturally, no one is in the pool or the hot tub for it is winter. How is this going to look on my obituary? **Frozen Flight Attendant found lifeless on the balcony of her hotel room in her long john's, Bronco sweatshirt and a dead cell phone!** I needed to get my adrenaline going and muster a few prayers for survival. I spotted a roof close by and took my chances with leaping over the railing. Wonder Woman would've been proud of my technique. Fortunately, I landed on my feet with no broken bones. Locating a maintenance door, I uttered another simple prayer for this to be open. Yay, for God's grace in my moment of crisis. I strolled down to the front desk in my pajamas, trying to catch my breath. When I approached the head clerk I requested, "I'm locked out of my room and need another key." He gazed at me in my outfit and clearly recognized my desperation replying, "I can assist you." I'm sure he thought I was a weird woman running around the hallways, not dressed in Victoria's Secret apparel by any means. *Like*

I care right now. Regardless, I headed back to my room with a sigh of relief. Sliding the card through the key slot, it opened, although I forgot I placed the safety latch over the door. This is a royal headache. Back to the front counter I sped and asked the same front desk clerk to contact maintenance. His look this time was one of concern. Maybe he thought I had a few "marbles loose", but he contacted a reliable staff member to get me back into my room. As I waited in front of my door still donned in my "jammies", I noticed a good size man coming down the hallway with tools dangling off his waistband. "What's your problem lady?" he inquired. I calmly expressed my situation. "Uh-huh" was his response. Within minutes, he managed to get my door open by using his knuckles to thrust in the right position to undo my safety latch. Despite the ridiculous process, I was elated to be back in my cozy spot.

Lesson 3: Take advantage of the extra security locks in your hotel room. You never know who may have access to your room due to a computer error when handing out room keys. Ladies, you can never be too trusting. Freddie Krueger might be lurking out yonder. Best to be safe than sorry.

Stranger danger is another topic of discussion. I was sound asleep in my room while in Texas, when suddenly I was awakened at midnight. My door opened up and the hallway light was flicked on. Someone stood for over fifteen minutes, never uttered a word and remained quiet. I was paralyzed with fear. Who's in my room? How did they get in? What do they want? I prayed in silence for protection. It was the longest span of time I can recall. The door finally closed. I jumped up to place a chair in front of my door, secured my safety latch, and grabbed any furniture in my room to block the door for security purposes. Since this episode I have been vigilant in retaining a watchful eye in my travels.

Lesson 4: Be thankful for the services rendered on behalf of our hotel accommodations and transportation provided to and from the airport's. They are working a job just like us and entail their fair share of mishaps. They have good days and unfortunate circumstances that arise. Be patient and appreciate all they provide for the sake of crew members.

Just like home you can have a few things erupt like a leaky faucet, over-flowing toilet, no hot water for your morning shower, hair dryers not working, heat or air-conditioning issues, or party animals whooping it up all night to disrupt your sleeping patterns. One hardship was when I was in Canada in December 2008. The temperature was forty-nine below zero without the wind chill. When I arrived into my room, the air-conditioning was still on. I contacted the front desk and they immediately sent maintenance to my room. This gentleman had to remove the panel to switch the mode to heat. I hung out in the hallway and eventually into the lobby, until my room warmed up. This took several hours for this to transpire due to an older hotel we were residing in. I finally trudged back to my room, tossed on a shower robe and shivered under the covers until my room maintained heat. It made me thankful for becoming warm again!

Then there is the extreme. In November of 2009, I was in the mountains at Colorado, a few days before Thanksgiving. I woke up at 3:30 in the morning feeling like a Butterball turkey in the oven. I noticed the temperature in my hotel room was ninety-seven degrees. I tried to turn off the heat, but it wouldn't shut off. In fact, it kept rising. I decided to open up the sliding glass door for some fresh air, although it was sealed for security purposes. Now I'm trying to blow-dry my hair for an early morning show time, yet sweat was dripping off my scalp. I desperately had to open my front door to allow some fresh air from the hallway to seep in before I passed out from the intense heat building up in my room. I couldn't wait to get to the lobby, even though I was an hour early for our van ride to the airport. How I needed some fresh air! When my fellow crew members, Captain Eric, and First Officer Alan, spotted me, they remarked "Why is your face so red? You look flushed Leenda. Are you running a fever or possibly encountering a hot flash?" My answer back to my loving co-workers was the following. "No my friends, I'm an over done stuffed turkey bird that has been gently cooked by the heat index in my room." They wanted to shove me in the nearest snow drift to cool off my over-heated body. Now that's what I consider true blue friends. Sometimes we take things for granted. When we indulge in a pool of whining or complaining is it worth the time nor energy? Have we lost our grip of appreciation when things don't go according to our comfort zone? I think so. Let's not dive into an instant gratification level, for it can be a short lived moment.

Lesson 5: If you don't have the time to pack a proper lunch for a trip series, capitalize on the free breakfast at the hotel you are staying in. It's a great perk. Make sure you have extra pockets to stock up on available treats. It comes in handy when you have no time to grab a bite to eat at the next airport to sustain your energy level!

Now here is the free food we enjoy. There's nothing better than to enjoy a complimentary breakfast or Manager's free grub they provide for their guests. My favorite memory of this topic was when I was in Savannah, Georgia. I headed down to the lobby and spotted my First Officer Mike dining on some chow. Simultaneously, there they were a great bunch of youngsters preparing for their sporting event in this area. Mike and I enjoyed our free meal, yet we filled our pockets with food to replenish our lunch pails. Strolling down the hallway you could hear a "swish." I resembled a kangaroo with banana's, muffins, cereal and bagel's dangling out of my trench coat! Gazing at my First Officer Mike, he had the same thing hanging out of his shorts. Being a quiet First Officer he remarked, "Can you tell we are crew members?" Giving him a nod I proposed, "Yes, but aren't we amazing when it comes to survival methods?"

Another episode was with Captain Aaron and First Officer Mike heading into Canada. Due to a late arrival none of us had an opportunity to eat. All restaurants were shut down, although our hotel provided us with a crew lounge. We were grade school children gathered on a picnic creating a midnight snack of peanut butter and jelly sandwiches, chips and a soda. We're not picky, yet seek a means to quench an empty belly.

Lesson 6: Wear your ear plugs at night to rest well and be aware of the nearest fire exits in case of a true emergency, whether or not it might be a false alarm.

We've all entailed lost sleep due to parties going all night, children running up and down the hallways playing tag, an occasional lovers quarrel next door, or "big foot" stomping back and forth above your room. We don't appreciate the disruptions, yet it happens. I'm sure hotel personnel witness the same craziness as crew members. They intend to grant every guest a good night's rest, but there's always a few mishaps. As an example, I was in Montana ready to bed down after a long day of traveling. I awoke to a blaring fire alarm in the early morning hours. I quickly escaped down the stair-well watching emergency doors block the corridor. With no make-up, hair spiked like a wheat crop, and flannels it was a pajama party outside the hotel in the middle of winter. I observed kids carrying their favorite pillows or stuffed animals, teenagers grasped their cell phones, business men held onto their lap-tops, while women clutched their purses. Obviously, these were the basic essentials to cling on to. Fire trucks, emergency responders and police officers circled the building. This turned out to be a fluke accident with the sensors at the hotel. Receiving a clearance to return to our rooms, the crowd scurried in a rapid pace to retain body heat. Naturally, I was wide awake and couldn't get back to sleep. When it was time to meet in the lobby for our ride to the airport, I asked Captain Steve, and First Officer Jared, "Where were you during the fire drill, for I searched for both of you?" They hesitated with an answer. Finally, Jared mentioned, "Oh heck, we opened up the door, never saw smoke so decided to head back to bed." *Hmmm, did I freak out due to a false alarm?* Maybe so, but I'd rather be prepared just in case it could be a true emergency.

Lesson 7: Revive your spirit

Take the time to explore your surroundings. It may not be "home sweet home", but utilize the duration of time as a learning tool to develop a sense of appreciation and gratitude. You can change turmoil into tranquility if you maintain a healthy attitude and a joyful spirit!

About the Author

As a freelance writer, Leenda has always loved to jot a note on a pad, napkin, or paper towel to remember and reflect on the everyday circumstances we contend with in life. Serving in the airline industry for over thirty-two years as a customer service agent, ramp agent, tour consultant, tour leader in Europe and USA for many airline companies, she came to a turning point in her seasoned years to begin a new career as a Flight Attendant. Many fascinating stories and true life experiences as an in-flight crew member compelled her to compose the following short stories.

She dedicates this book to her fellow in-flight friends, especially her Denver-based crew members, administration, and ground personnel. Despite many setbacks with short-lived dreams in several jobs, they have been a true brilliant light in believing in her talent as a writer. She will be eternally grateful for their encouraging words, support, and perseverance of seeing this come to print after many hard years of labor and keen observation. Their journeys together while *Lost in the Clouds* is an inspirational, courageous, and humorous version of what they entail on the ground as well as in the air. If she begins to lose her Irish sense of humor in tackling her job in the aviation business, then it's time to toss in the polyester uniform. To laugh is a gift to share with others. The short stories she has written are based on true in-flight incidents. The name of the company and individual names may have been altered to protect the innocent who chose not to be mentioned. Her intention in designing this series of short stories is to make you giggle. She hopes you enjoy, understand, and form a deeper appreciation of what crew members undergo while on duty. In closing, they are a "whomp-pomp-a-loop-a" group.

"Lost in the Clouds" is an every- day compilation of short story encounters in life from sea-level to thirty-three thousand feet in the sky. From the break of dawn to the splendor of a sunset, we may find ourselves lost in the clouds; however, the mysterious power of God protects the soul through peace and joy, illuminating light through human connection.

I am forever indebted to being closer to heaven and Him while providing a platform to serve as a Flight Attendant, along with my fellow crew members and passengers. Through these encounters, we feel the embellishment of the Holy Spirit.

Remember God is good!

Psalm 36: 9, For with you is the fountain of life;
Your light we shall see.

CPSIA information can be obtained
at www.ICGtesting.com
Printed in the USA
BVOW08s0340230118
505500BV00002B/112/P